Don't Get Mad...
Get Even!

Don't Get Mad... Get Even!

A Manual for Retaliation

by
ALAN ABEL

Illustrations by
SIMON BOND

W. W. NORTON & COMPANY
NEW YORK   LONDON

Copyright © 1983 by Spencer Productions, Inc.
Illustrations Copyright © 1983 by Simon Bond
Published simultaneously in Canada by George J. McLeod
Limited, Toronto.

Printed in the United States of America

All Rights Reserved
First Edition

Library of Congress Cataloging in Publication Data

Abel, Alan.
   Don't get mad—get even!

   1. Revenge—Anecdotes, facetiae, satire, etc.
I. Bond, Simon.   II. Title.
BF637.R48A24 1983   158'.2   82–14352

ISBN 0-393-01614-5

ISBN 0-393-30118-4 PBK.

W. W. Norton & Company, Inc., 500 Fifth Avenue, New York,
N.Y. 10110
W. W. Norton & Company Ltd., 37 Great Russell Street,
London WC1B 3NU

Book design by Jacques Chazaud
Manufactured by the Haddon Craftsmen, Inc.

1 2 3 3 4 5 6 7 8 9 0

To Jeanne and Jennifer

Contents

8 ·

Introduction

Are you living longer but enjoying it less? Because you've been shafted by someone today? And you're sulking in front of the TV set with a pile of junk food to numb the pain?

Well, you're going to be rejected, assaulted, or intimidated again tomorrow and for the rest of your unnatural life! You can quietly suffer or shout: "I'm not going to take it anymore and I intend to get even!"

The rejectors, assaulters, and intimidators are everywhere in power. Like cockroaches, they outlive fine and fragile human specimens. They're dedicated to demeaning you by destroying your peace of mind.

Have you already had enough aggravation in life? Fine. Join the club. Now use that frustration to turn your psyche completely around. *Don't get mad . . . get even!*

Start by taking this book to the cashier and paying the price. It's worth it. Otherwise, please put my twenty years of expertise back on the shelf in a more prominent position.

Alan Abel

New York, N.Y.
May 1, 1982

Acknowledgments ▬▬▬▬▬▬

To all those friends and acquaintances who suggested ideas, many of which were not printable, my thanks to them in alphabetical disorder: Anne Gibson, Steve Singer, Lee Carlson, David Dawson, Donna White, Walter Evans, Ray Williams, Kathy Brennan, Debi Kops, Bob Blumenblatt, Gene Buck, Corrine Holden, Jim Porter, Chris Krycinski, Aaron Leventhal, Jack Milton, Sam Ballin, Doug Quin, Carolyn Conrad, Lee Chirillo, Ken Conner, Milt Shefter, Deborah Harmon, and Tom Laird.

Don't Get Mad...
Get Even!

How to Avoid Tipping ▬▬▬▬▬

Most people object to tipping even when the service is good. But the outstretched palm of a rude waiter deserves to be slapped, not greased with money. (Be careful. In French restaurants a slap is still considered a challenge to duel!)

I propose we stop tipping until employers hire dedicated people and pay them a decent wage commensurate with their services. Until then, here are a few ways to save money and avoid an embarrassing scene.

When riding in a taxi, casually mention that you are unemployed and three months behind on your rent, telephone, and insurance payments. The driver will not expect a tip because he likes to feel sorry for someone worse off than he is.

If the cab's destination is a hotel, be prepared to face a gauntlet of tipping threats. First, the doorman. He will rush to the taxi, open the door halfway, and block your exit until you reach for your wallet. Pretend you are nearsighted and leave quickly by the other side.

Once inside the hotel, *run* through the lobby to the desk so as to escape greedy bellmen waiting in ambush. Usually their uniforms match the decor, making them invisible.

When checking in, allow the desk clerk to see a small length of chain around your wrist that disappears into a suitcase. If he or she summons a bellhop, confide that you are a special courier with strict orders to carry your own bags. It works like a charm because everybody loves a spy.

Inside your room there will be a planned absence of clean towels, soap, and facial tissues. Calling the maid would involve a tip. Instead, seek out her cart on the floor and help yourself to the necessary items.

Next, you'll need a hotel engineer because the television isn't working properly, the heat or air conditioning remain silent, and a lightbulb is missing. Don't be fooled by his friendly, soft-spoken manner. He expects a sizable tip and reminds you of this by mentioning the four kids in college.

Don't panic. Dangle your arm helplessly from the elbow and talk about the costly operations you've endured to correct this malfunction. He's bound to sympathize and not expect a gratuity.

Down in the hotel dining room, give the maître d's hand a firm shake and compliment him on how pleased you are to meet. This homespun approach will distract his attention from receiving funds and he will dismiss you as a naïve rube.

For the unattentive waiter or waitress, I suggest leaving a printed card on the table after eating as follows:

I DID NOT LEAVE A TIP BECAUSE

_____You forgot the fingerbowl.
_____The drinking glass was dirty.
_____You were conspicuous by your absence.
_____Your appearance is unappetizing.
_____The food was not cooked properly.
_____God will bless you for your service.

Don't check anything off. It's more fun that way. (Warning! Wear a disguise if you return to this restaurant. Otherwise, you'll get a wobbly table by the kitchen where guerrilla-trained busboys rattle huge trays of dirty dishes perilously over your head.)

Generally speaking, tipping should be reserved for exemplary service and discontinued as a mandatory handout. When waiters and other employees start complaining loudly enough to be heard in the boss's office, where he's counting his profits, they might receive a better base salary.

The Insolent Clerk ▬▬▬▬▬

Who hasn't been insulted by a nasty store clerk in front of customers? And you can't think of a single comeback except to disappear quickly. Once out on the street you devise all kinds of brilliant retaliations. But it's too late.

The dirty bird who insults you publicly deserves to be kicked mentally for bad manners. It's not good for the store's business or your ego.

A few years ago I started my own recording company and decided to visit Poughkeepsie, New York, to promote an instrumental novelty, "Poughkeepsie Pizzicato."

The first record store I approached had several customers and I waited patiently. When the lady clerk came to me, I explained I only needed five minutes. She threw up her hands in disgust, uttered several derogatory remarks, and waited on other people.

After forty-five minutes, with more customers entering, she finally turned to me and shouted, "Out! I don't want any record salesmen in the store today. Get out, now!"

I started for the door and hesitated. She picked up a broom and waved it menacingly. So I left.

Standing outside, terribly annoyed at this lack of hospitality in the hometown of Vassar College, a customer who had witnessed the outburst came over. He explained I had tangled with the wife of the owner. Apparently she became a tyrant when her husband was away.

I found another record store to handle my line and drove back to New York steaming from the unwarranted eviction. If I protested, it was her property and she could have had me arrested for unlawful loitering.

Still burning a few days later, I decided to state my objections in a letter to the owner.

Manager
Record Store
Poughkeepsie, New York

Dear Sir:

By way of introduction I was in your store last week to present my records while you were gone. The clerk on duty would not permit me to leave any samples. Instead, I was thrown out!

I didn't get the clerk's name but I can describe her and I feel she should be severely reprimanded for obnoxious behavior.

She had red stringy hair, a rather dumpy figure, was grossly made up, sloppily dressed, and reeking from the odor of cheap perfume.

I trust you will be able to finger this employee and deliver the proper denunciation for her despicable manners.

Yours very truly,
Alan Abel

Several days after sending the letter I received an angry phone call:

"That was my wife you insulted! We're going to sue you!"

I told him I wasn't concerned about a lawsuit because I had described her rather accurately. He hung up on me. I felt I had gotten even.

Pushy Panhandlers

Hostile street beggars are a blight on society and many of them earn as much, if not more, than corporate executives. They don't pay taxes (the panhandlers, that is), have very little overhead, and no inventory or credit losses.

Some are particularly adept at cornering couples and intimidating the male companion. Saying "no" will only egg them on to becoming quite belligerent. It's sidewalk blackmail.

To avoid this annoying breed of leech, especially when you suspect the panhandler is better off than you are, consider the following ploys:

1. Become ill instantly and ask to borrow his or her scarf, hat, or handkerchief.
2. Pretend to be drunk and babble some nonsense as you stagger away.
3. Quickly take off your wristwatch and offer to sell it to the beggar for a fast $25. If a sale is about to be made, mention that it's part of a package deal and must be purchased with your cufflinks and fountain pen. That will kill the sale and you won't be bothered further.
4. Speak only in French or any other language you have a slight knowledge of.

This last gimmick backfired once when the seedy-looking tramp answered me fluently. I gave him a dollar.

First-Class Seats at Economy Prices

Ever since slavery was abolished one would think we were finished with the caste system. But airlines still practice it. First class gets you wider seats, more leg room, better food, free liquor, and bigger smiles from the stewardesses.

I resent this double standard in America as I sit in economy class, strapped upright like a salami with a talkative person on my left exhaling garlic fumes and a large gorilla type on my right wheezing cold germs.

We're all so close we could be arrested for molesting one another! And when the food trays arrive I must endure a ridiculous cramped ritual of aiming toy food particles straight up to my mouth.

Then I notice other three-seat sections with only one or two people. Why did the diabolical airline clerk sentence me to this torture? Can't I at least suffer in silence?

Blabbermouth on my left recites his track record selling heavy farm machinery. The incredible hulk to the right, making his first air trip, "whoops" loudly at every slight air turbulence. He also has a nervous habit of gripping my arm in fear.

I remind the fearful one that people in first class are more likely to die if we crash, because in a nose dive they're closer to the ground. He reaches for the airsickness bag. I take the opportunity to change seats.

In the future, anyone can avoid such situations by flying "first class" in the coach section if you're willing to utilize the following suggestions:

1. Sit in a "no smoking" seat early and place an unlit cigarette, cigar, or pipe in your mouth.
2. Make visible a package of Mail Pouch chewing tobacco.

3. Leave four or five panels of toilet tissue on the adjacent seats.

4. Hold an open airsickness bag in front of your face.

People assigned to your row will make immediate arrangements to move. By employing techniques #3 and #4 on a recent jam-packed flight to Pittsburgh, I had the only three-seat row to myself!

Also, to maintain a private row of seats, you can talk quietly to yourself, keep a thumb in your mouth, or laugh audibly every thirty seconds until the passengers sit elsewhere.

Should you end up with a companion who wants to bend your ears senselessly, the best way to cut him or her off is to mention your profession: you're an embalmer. Or you work for a syndicate on "special hit contracts" to take care of certain enemies. And you are on your way to rub out someone as a favor to a friend.

When asked what the intended victim has done to deserve his fate, mention casually, "Oh, he just talks all the time; a real nuisance."

This latter tale will muzzle the most garrulous types imaginable.

An all-purpose technique for maintaining total solitude, while traveling on public carriers, is to place a piece of string in your mouth and allow it to dangle. Nobody likes to sit near or talk to a stranger with a string hanging from his lips.

Diabolical Dunners

Probably the most aggravating mail is being received from credit-card companies, department stores, and firms that offer installment buying.

Inevitably, there is an uncredited payment, a stranger's expense billed to your account, or an unwarranted finance charge that continues to show on monthly statements.

This anonymous enemy is destined to upset your equilibrium the first of every month. I suggest a form letter to handle these irritants:

Dear Writer_____ Creditor_____ Other_____:

_____ I will not respond until I receive a personally typed explanation in simple English along with documented evidence.

_____ A copy of my complaint has been sent to your superior.

_____ Only under very extraordinary circumstances do I respond to someone beneath my station in life.

_____ Based on reports from my graphologist, you do not qualify.

_____ Your poor penmanship suggests you are an alien. I have asked the Department of Immigration to investigate.

_____ I have filed a complaint with the _____ Better Business Bureau _____ Chamber of Commerce _____ Federal Trade Commission _____ Securities and Exchange Commission _____ Supt. of Banks.

_____ In the light of your poor bookkeeping, I have asked the Internal Revenue Service to conduct a full field audit of your company.

_____ A person with your demonic mentality could represent a national security threat to our elected public officials. Therefore, I have notified the Secret Service.

_____ I have come across a few incompetent idiots, but you take the cake!

Good-bye Forever

Form letters are most useful when replying to some offensive person who won't take "no" for an answer.

Dear_____

_____I don't like you.

_____I don't need you.

_____I don't want you.

_____I hate you.

_____Our relationship is hereby terminated forthwith throughout the world in perpetuity.

_____If you contact me one more time I shall notify:

_____the police _____Your mother

_____Your wife _____Your husband.

_____I intend to print your phone number on the wall of every public john.

_____The blisters have been determined to be:

_____cold sores _____scabies _____herpes.

_____I don't know what I'll do without you, but I'd rather.

_____If you were the only person left in the world, fine. Until then, please get lost!

Offensive Customs Inspectors

The Customs agent is the scourge of the earth. I doubt if any has ever won a Dale Carnegie or Horatio Alger award.

I have endured their clumsiness when an inspector dropped and broke my quart of whisky, their selfishness (seizing my lone Cuban cigar), and being unduly interrogated along with a complete baggage search.

Other travelers have spent an hour or more while a suspicious agent dumps all their belongings and paws through everything, forcing them to miss travel connections.

Meantime, the real criminals such as drug kingpins, slush-fund carriers, and jewel thieves waltz right through to carry on their business as usual. The guardians of our shores continually scrutinize the wrong people with high-handed rudeness.

I've been able to overcome the Customs offensiveness by using a tape recorder. This conversation on my return from London should demonstrate a method for others who resent being tagged as an unsavory suspect:

"Do you have anything to declare?"

"Only the gifts represented by these receipts totaling $137.75."

"Let's put your bags up here and open them."

"Fine. I'd like to record this inspection, with your permission. I'm a writer and the experience should help with an article I'll be writing for a national magazine."

"I would not like to be recorded."

"As you wish. Then I'll just record my conversation and leave yours out. Agent Jones is opening my briefcase, carefully noting its contents to make certain there are no secret plans for overthrowing our government or evidence of illegal drugs, firearms, and other contraband that might be in violation of laws involving an American citizen returning from overseas. Agent Jones has decided not to examine my two suitcases and I am free to enter the United States of America with a clean bill of health."

I have used the tape machine to and from the United States on numerous occasions with only a cursory Customs look at my luggage.

My First Retaliation

My first chance to get even happened on the campus of Ohio State University where I presented jazz concerts. When the late bandleader Gene Krupa unexplicably canceled a sold-out appearance, I tracked him down to a nearby resort hotel.

Krupa said he was exhausted from one-night stands and refused to honor the engagement. He intended to stay in his room and rest. I left, faced with the prospect of refunding 1500 admissions the next day. But a plan began to form in my mind.

Early the following morning I showed up at his hotel with six campus beauties and they persuaded a bellman to open Krupa's door, explaining it was a surprise birthday party.

Krupa was still in bed and half-dazed when the girls, singing "Happy Birthday," hustled him into a suit and dragged the protesting star drummer down to a waiting caravan of convertibles. A dixieland band played loudly as students waved signs reading "HAPPY BIRTHDAY GENE KRUPA!" and "WELCOME TO OHIO STATE UNIVERSITY."

During the hour ride to the college, I sat next to Krupa as he denied it was his birthday and planned to sue me and the university, and press kidnapping charges. Furthermore, he didn't intend to play a single drumbeat.

Arriving at University Hall on campus, he was dragged into a backstage dressing room by the girls and kept under guard until the afternoon concert. I contacted his musicians at the same resort hotel by phone and they agreed to hurry over with their instruments for the surprise birthday party.

At concert time, with the band set up on stage, Krupa was carried out and placed behind his drums. He sat there belligerently as the audience rose to its feet applauding wildly.

Prior to the bandleader's unusual entrance, I had quietly warned the packed auditorium that Gene Krupa felt he was no longer admired by his fans, after a bum marijuana conviction, and would need tumultuous applause to break the spell.

Krupa gradually smiled and started playing a tom-tom introduction to "Sing, Sing, Sing." The musicians joined in and an exciting two-hour concert followed that remains a historic event on the Ohio State University campus.

Afterward, Krupa asked me to become his personal manager. I declined the offer, but we remained lifelong friends.

If at First You Don't Succeed

During the early 1950s, I arrived in New York with a music degree and the determination to fulfill my lifelong ambition: as percussionist with the *Radio City Music Hall* Orchestra.

Drumsticks in hand, I found the Music Hall stage door and announced to orchestra manager Joe Saunders that I was ready for an audition. He shook his head sadly and showed me a list of eighteen drummers on call.

"In fifteen years we've only had to use the top ten," he explained with some annoyance. "You don't stand a chance."

"But I have a college degree from Ohio State University," I argued. "And experience with the Columbus Symphony, David Rose, Sauter-Finnegan. . . ."

"Sorry," he interrupted. "There are no auditions today, tomorrow, or ever."

Utterly defeated and depressed, I walked the streets for

hours. All the years practicing and performing to achieve my ultimate fantasy went down the drain in ten miserable minutes.

I called Saunders several weeks later asking for a second chance. He came right to the point.

"Your unlucky number is nineteen. Now let's terminate this relationship."

Weeks of gloom went by while I played drums weekends with Lester Lanin's society orchestra and practiced hours in a tiny room less than a mile from Radio City.

When I voiced my frustration to a drummer friend and psychologist, Dr. Robert Topper, he advised me to consider some sort of persuasive action. But not to give up trying.

I responded to his encouragement by printing 100 postcards with my professional experience and telephone number. Every single day I mailed one to Joe Saunders.

At the end of ten weeks he had received, and undoubtedly destroyed, seventy postal reminders of my availability. I avoided walking anywhere near Radio City Music Hall.

One morning, an hour before showtime, drummer Billy Gladstone called in sick. Saunders frantically tapped his list of eighteen standbys. He was phoning number twelve without success—it was then forty minutes until the overture—and the morning mail arrived with postcard #96.

In a moment of diabolical rage, Saunders dialed my number and with teeth clenched asked if I could be at the theater in ten minutes. I shouted "Yes!" and took off.

With kaleidoscopic frenzy, I knocked over a lamp, grabbed my favorite sticks, flew down six flights of stairs, hailed a taxi, and made it to the orchestra pit in fourteen minutes.

Somebody handed me a jacket and tie, I adjusted the drums, and acknowledged a nervous wink from conductor Raymond Paige.

Joe Saunders stood in the wings, arms folded, face grimacing, waiting for the moment I goofed so he could personally

throw me out. Another substitute drummer had been reached and was due to arrive momentarily.

Sightreading being one of my stronger assets, I sailed through the opening music without missing a cue. After the overture, Maestro Paige gave me a positive high sign and Saunders disappeared with his standby drummer.

When this first show ended, the conductor and musicians were full of congratulations. Joe Saunders, wiping his brow and shaking his head in disbelief at the turn of events, offered a limp handshake.

I continued to play regularly at Radio City Music Hall because I refused to get mad and, instead, got even.

How to Manufacture a Recording Contract

As an undergraduate student in music, I wrote a number of compositions for percussion ensembles. The sight and sound of six drummers playing melodies on tympani, bells, xylophones, and chimes was quite a novelty. And when the Ohio State University Marching Band featured our "Serenade to a Sand Dune" during a halftime show, they received the greatest reception ever.

This experiment with percussive jazz seemed like a good recording concept, and after graduation I submitted tapes to various record companies without any success.

The rejections were cordial enough. Several artistic directors suggested they might be interested if and when we made a name in the concert field.

This comment is standard from agents, producers, and

managers; that is, "go out and become famous, then we'll consider acquiring your talents."

It's a real Catch-22 and every performer knows this as he or she struggles valiantly just to work at a chosen profession, let alone become rich and famous!

Rather than form a percussion ensemble and endure the rigors of playing concerts on the road, I put some ingenuity to use and former experience as a travel counselor for the American Automobile Association.

Utilizing a collection of maps, I booked an imaginary tour of thirty major United States cities by "The First Percussion Sextet." Then I created a series of glowing press reviews covering some of the "concerts."

Once a week I mailed the press releases to record companies and kept my fingers crossed. The sixth week's mailing brought a call from RCA's George Avakian. He was ready to record our ensemble and wanted to arrange a date in two weeks!

Looking at my pinpointed "tour" map, I blindly selected West Virginia University in Morgantown. Avakian agreed to schedule a remote recording unit there on the designated Sunday. We would meet the next day to sign a contract.

I had ten days to get this act together. Otherwise it meant blowing a lucrative launching with a major record company for a concept I knew intuitively had mass marketing appeal.

Luck and timing play a crucial role in cementing creative elements. It didn't help to have put the cart before the horse, but there was no other way.

I called Dr. Joseph Gluck, chairman of the West Virginia University Music Department. Fortunately, he was delighted to receive a percussion concert two weeks away with RCA recording the event.

Next step, forming a percussion sextet! With the assistance of Radio City Music Hall tympanist Bob Swan and Broadway show percussionist Warren Hard, we rounded up a group of top-notch drummers. Arrangers Norman Leyden and Norman Beatty wrote some additional music and a week of frantic rehearsing completed that phase.

We gave the concert before an enthusiastic audience in Morgantown, West Virginia, and RCA Victor released the first of two albums that led to appearances on the "Ed Sullivan Show," "Today," and "I've Got a Secret."

There were many offers to tour the ensemble but I turned them down. Enough was enough! I had gotten satisfaction.

Taxpayer vs. IRS

The Internal Revenue Service chose to audit my tax returns and I relished the opportunity to spar with these underpaid, overbearing government servants.

Gathering all books, records, and cancelled checks, I went to their command post at 90 Church Street in New York City. The 9:00 A.M. appointment was honored at 11:30 and by noon the agent stopped for lunch.

During the afternoon session there was one trying moment when the examiner spotted an expenditure of $386.75 "to see Mike Douglas." He didn't feel I could "visit a fellow and deduct the costs." I surmised he never owned a television set and he didn't. Another agent was called in to rule in my favor.

Promptly at 5:00 P.M. I was dismissed with a clean bill of health. I thought about the full day wasted to satisfy the evil eye of a government watchdog who wasn't even a certified public accountant. And I wondered if an honest taxpayer could examine *their* books and records to satisfy his curiosity where all the money went.

Maverick attorney Roger Jon Diamond, from Pacific Palisades, California, filed my suit in federal court demanding that the United States government bring all its cancelled checks for the previous year to Lafayette Park in Washington, D.C., where I would spot-check expenditures.

Uncle Sam assigned a dozen lawyers to fight our action. I was harassed with daily depositions under oath, until the fourth session that went as follows:

"Mr. Abel, would you explain one of your professional activities in detail."

"Well, I practice with these drumsticks and I'll demonstrate. There are twenty-six rudiments, thirty if you include the flam paradiddle-diddle, the three-stroke roll, the triple ratamacue, and the seventeen-stroke roll."

I then proceeded to spend hours playing thirty snare drum rudiments, allowing ten minutes to explain and develop each one at different tempos and dynamics. An exasperated stenographer went batty trying to transcribe the sounds. The government lawyers canceled all further hearings.

We lost the first round in court when the presiding judge ruled that my case was "of frivolous merits" and did not deserve to go to trial.

I could have appealed but felt satisfied with the resultant press coverage. Reporters had a field day with this unusual case.

The following year, guess what? I was called in for another tax audit.

Armed with my documents and wired for sound—just in case—I appeared promptly for the examination. Two agents met me at the door, I was greeted warmly by name, gently ushered into a grand office, served coffee and doughnuts, and seated on a very comfortable chair.

A quick check by one of the men showed I might owe the government $36.

"Forget it," he said. "It's not worth the paperwork."

Forty minutes later I was on my way home. Apparently, my tax return was selected from a random computer search. But they didn't really want to tangle with me again.

How to Evict a Reluctant Roommate

I had moved into a three-room furnished apartment and was surprised to see men's clothing and golf clubs in the closet. The front door opened suddenly and in walked Harry, wearing a smartly tailored airline pilot's uniform.

He apologized for the intrusion, explaining he was the former tenant, but his new apartment furniture hadn't arrived. Could he stay for a week or two and share the rent? Furthermore, with his busy flight schedule, I would only see him on weekends.

Harry impressed me with his charming manner and I saw no objection to this arrangement. He changed clothes and said he would return very late in the evening.

About 3:00 A.M. I awakened, smelling smoke. Dashing into Harry's room, I saw the window curtains burning; he was fast asleep with cigarette butts all over the floor. Dousing the flames with water, I tried to awaken him. Harry grumbled, turned over, and went on sleeping.

The next day we had a confrontation. He promised to replace the curtains and said it would never happen again. But Harry performed the same set-fire-to-the-curtains routine over the next three weekends.

I ordered him to leave immediately. He refused and pleaded for another chance, claiming his nerves were still shattered from flying missions during the Korean War.

Meantime, he was shattering my nerves. The landlord listened to my complaint and responded, "I wanted him out for the same reason; he's a split personality, flying planes by day, setting fires at night. Legally it's your apartment, but we'll have to go to court for an eviction notice that will take six months, maybe longer."

Harry's fires were always small ones, not large enough to call the fire department. Nor could I involve the police because they would have to catch him in the act.

I called my psychologist friend Dr. Robert Topper, and he offered a plan:

"It sounds like you've inherited a psychopathic pyromaniac and he *likes* you. The only way to get him out is to create a false eviction for *both* of you."

The landlord was willing to cooperate and mailed us a notice to evacuate the premises within forty-eight hours as "undesirable tenants."

Harry wanted to hire a lawyer and fight. I insisted we just leave peacefully. Reluctantly, he checked into a hotel and I stayed overnight with a friend. Then I changed the locks and moved back in.

Several weeks later Harry called out of curiosity and was furious at my deception. I just thanked him for moving because I wanted to live safely and happily ever after.

As a footnote to this incident, I had reported his actions to an airline supervisor and he branded me a troublemaker "because Harry makes the most beautiful touchdowns at New York's JFK Airport and doesn't show a single blemish on his flying record."

A year later Harry made the mistake of setting fire to his

hotel room on an overnight flight to Denver. He was subsequently fired.

Everytime I fly, I look inside the cockpit to check out the pilot's and co-pilot's faces. Just in case.

Clobbering Crooked Tenants

My friend Sam was a widower who retired to Florida. Instead of selling his furnished home on Long Island, he decided to rent it for a year to a nice young couple. The income would help with mortgage payments on his condominium overlooking the ocean in Fort Lauderdale.

When the rental money stopped arriving after nine months and the phone was disconnected, Sam returned home to investigate. The couple had invited a family of four to move in and they abused many of his furnishings. Neighbors reported all-night noisy, drunken parties, and on occasion had called the police to restore order.

He was angry and depressed. The tenants claimed to be on welfare, had no money to pay further rent, and intended to stay entrenched forever.

Sam considered legal eviction, a long and costly process with the courts generously allowing the occupants to remain on the premises. He would lose income and they could continue destroying his home with fiendish delight.

I suggested he hire a moving van and six beefy actors to remove every stick of furniture. Two of the meaner looking men would pose as new owners, flash a bill of sale, and order the poachers out in no uncertain terms.

It worked. Sam got his house back over a weekend, losing only one month's rent and $450 for the fake moving. But he saved thousands of dollars in legal fees and untold hours of grief.

When to Play Doctor

Public servants generally respect medical people. Any other average person, regardless of his profession, is just a sheep in line begging for service.

To retaliate against this injustice and save valuable time, I always use "Dr. Abel" when making reservations for dining, airline tickets, or hotel accommodations. The preferential treatment is marvelous to behold.

When ordering hotel room service, my medical prefix ensures prompt delivery. The conversation usually goes like this:

"Dr. Abel in Room 537. Could I please have my breakfast in twenty minutes? I'm due at the hospital in forty."

"Certainly, doctor. I'll handle your order personally."

Being a night owl, and often having checked in late the evening before, I find hotel and motel noon checkout times a real nuisance. A call to the assistant manager, explaining the urgency for three more hours to complete my medical report, provides the leisurely exodus I prefer.

In many motels, the manager, desk clerk, and switchboard operator are one person. If he or she is reluctant to extend the checkout time without charge, I cite the Federal Occupancy Law whereby a guest must receive a minimum of

twenty hours' room residency.

I made the law up, but it sounds plausible and an employee hesitates to admit ignorance. So I'm given the extra room time.

On occasion I've had to travel between three different cities the same day for television appearances on a very tight schedule. Grabbing an immediate taxi at the airports becomes a necessity and a problem with several dozen people in line ahead.

My solution is to wear a medical jacket and stethoscope. The starter gives me preference for the first cab and I can meet the critical deadlines.

While shooting a movie in Boston, our camera crew ran out of film. An early-morning call to Eastman Kodak in Rochester assured us that two boxes of film would arrive on the noon bus.

However, the package terminal supervisor told my production assistant to return at 3:00 P.M. because his six workers were on their lunch hour. She pleaded in vain as he went back to picking his teeth and telling bawdy jokes, amid hundreds of boxes in huge piles.

Paying our twelve crewmen and six actors for three extra hours would have taken us over budget. So I donned my white jacket and squeezed a splotch of ketchup on the front.

Storming into the package room, I loudly demanded to know who was in charge. Without waiting for a reply, I shouted:

"I've got a patient on the table hemorrhaging. The blood plasma came from Rochester labeled motion picture film to prevent it from being stolen. I want it right now! Move!"

All seven of the rough and tumble guys scrambled like

Keystone Cops in a Mack Sennett comedy. It didn't take them a minute to find the shipment.

As I left, I said, "Thanks, fellows. Maybe you'll appreciate this service if you ever find yourselves in a similar emergency."

Practically in unison, they all shouted, "Good luck, doc. Hope you save the patient."

Uninvited House Guests ▬▬▬▬▬

When I first moved to the country for peace and quiet, I was bombarded with visits from long-forgotten relatives and former fair-weather friends.

Although my house was well hidden at the dead-end of a treacherous dirt road, strategically mined with axle-crunching pot holes, everybody found it quite easily and explained, "We just happened to be driving by."

Not even Rex, my snarling great dane, frothing at the mouth (I put Bromo Seltzer in his water dish) was a deterrent.

One cousin I never knew arrived overnight to borrow a few dollars for an important business deal in Ireland. When I refused, he disappeared before dawn along with my best green tie.

A few days later, while mowing the lawn, a woman showed up and introduced herself as an aunt who knew me when I was six months old. She could only stay for dinner and a few pieces of silverware.

Desperate for some solitude, I placed a scarlet fever quarantine sign on the front fence. One nosy neighbor came over to investigate, claiming she had received all the necessary shots before going to Europe and was immune to me. I treated her the same way until she left.

To discourage uninvited house guests, I devised a questionnaire and placed copies on an end table in the foyer. Nearby is a writing desk with a chained ballpoint pen I purchased at a post office auction. A sign requests that each visitor fill in this form completely:

1. Name, last known address, and relationship to me, if any.
2. What is the purpose of this visit?
3. How long do you expect to stay?
4. Are there any particular foods you can't eat?
5. Whom should I notify in case of illness?
6. Weight of your baggage on arrival:_____
   On departing: _____ (Use scale in bathroom.)

Welcome to a brief stay at Withered Pines and I look forward to your safe journey home. Meantime, please observe the following:

1. If you wake up at night, frightened by strange, eerie sounds, please muffle your screams so as not to disturb other sleepers.
2. At the sound of three bells, join me promptly in the attic for a seance with my great-grandfather.
3. *No smoking in bed.* In case of fire, there is a knotted rope under the bed. Be sure to tie one end securely around something strong before climbing down. *Random fire drills will be held between midnight and dawn.*
4. You will find a wide variety of cigarettes, candy, and soft drinks in the pantry. (Machines take quarters, nickels, or dimes.)
5. Breakfast is served between 5:00 A.M. and 5:30 A.M. only,

followed by group calisthenics on the front lawn. *Nobody will be excused without a medical permit.*

It is once again peaceful in the country. The only uninvited guests now are bees, birds, crickets, and locusts; they are welcome to stay as long as they wish.

Intrusive Sunday Visitors ━━━━

Sunday, your day of rest. Forget it. The ringing phone at 8:00 A.M. signals a family of four coming to say "hello" around lunchtime. Always the diplomat, you explain, "Gee, Henry, we won't be home. . . . We're leaving for a trip to . . . ah, the zoo."

Henry says they'll drop by anyhow to return the books he borrowed last year and hide them in your garage, if you'll keep the door open.

Now you have to play hide and seek. The car is parked around the block. A note pinned on the door thanks Henry for returning the books. To sound a warning alarm, one lookout is appointed just before noon. Then everybody hides in the bedroom. Let the phone ring and there should be no talking, coughing, laughing, or sneezing.

Henry and family will come and go with your friendship remaining intact. However, some Sunday visitors arrive unexpectedly without calling first. Have your slide collection ready and announce two hours of vacation photographs with a personal narration.

I keep 2000 slides in a huge box for such an occasion. Unannounced visitors can generally stand about twenty minutes of the Grand Canyon, Disneyland, and Pikes Peak be-

fore realizing they have an important engagement elsewhere.

Another good ploy is to put on some dirty clothes and invite your well-dressed guests to join you in an old-fashioned house-cleaning party. Offer ragged garments for all and then watch everybody disappear.

Borrowing without Collateral

Ten years ago I was at my wit's end trying to raise $10,000 for a pilot film that could be expanded to feature length. A potential backer had promised that if he liked what he saw, the six-figure sum to complete the movie would be mine.

There was a three-month time limit and it sailed by as I went through our savings attempting to persuade friends, relatives, and business contacts to invest. From their standpoint, I was a poor risk without a track record in filmmaking.

I thought about loan sharks and called a former acquaintance who worked on the docks. Tino knew several but wouldn't help me because I'd end up in a cement suit.

The complete shooting script was sitting on my desk and I toyed with the idea of just dropping it into the waste basket along with the morning mail.

One advertising piece from Bankers Trust Company was signed by the board chairman. Why not write him for a loan?

Mr. William Moore, Chairman
Bankers Trust Company
16 Wall Street
New York, NY 10005

Dear Mr. Moore:

By way of introduction I am unemployed, have no savings, stocks, bonds, or real estate . . . except for a small sliver of land in Manhattan I bought at public auction for $25 (measuring 1 ft. by 2 in.) and donated to the Indians as a symbolic redemption.

Nevertheless, I would like to request an unsecured loan of $10,000 to begin shooting a motion picture film. As security, I can offer my integrity and the following collateral endorsements:

1. My wife and I have lived in the same apartment for ten years without a single complaint from our neighbors. Nor have I ever missed paying the rent.
2. As a loyal customer of your bank for ten years, I have never had a check bounce.
3. I have stood in line at Bankers Trust for over an hour without creating a disturbance, was never rude to any of your tellers, or ever dropped a soiled deposit slip on the floor.
4. As anxious as I am for this money, I would never consider robbing any of your branches.
5. If a stranger on the street were to ask me to recommend a reliable bank, I would always say, "Try Bankers Trust."
6. As a former member of the armed forces, I was pleased to defend America against foreign enemies who would have prevented Bankers Trust from operating as a free enterprise.

Hoping this information is sufficient to extend yourself, I remain

Respectfully yours,
Alan Abel

I sent the letter because when you're down and out with your back to the wall, the only chance is to fire a well-aimed long shot. It's also good for mental therapy.

Three days later I received a call from my Bankers Trust branch manager. He informed me I had $10,000 in my checking account!

As I learned much later, Mr. Moore's secretary read the letter and passed it along to him for a morning laugh to start the day. He appreciated my sardonic humor and okayed the loan personally.

The pilot film pleased my backer and *Is There Sex After Death?*, an R-rated satire, was finished within its budget.

How to Invite a Reluctant V.I.P.

After completing *Is There Sex After Death?* I had one print and no distributor. The major film moguls offered to screen the movie in the privacy of their homes, but this was a risky procedure. There would be no audience reaction in someone's living room and the print might be damaged, lost, or stolen.

So I set a screening date at the prestigious Rizzoli Screening Room in New York City and called the major film distributors with a plea to attend.

Every secretary responded similarly: "Mr. V.I.P. does not attend screenings; you'll have to send the film over and take your chances."

I made one gamble and delivered the film to Columbia Pictures. A week later I retrieved it from their projectionist who said the chief executive watched the opening titles, received a phone call, and left, never to return!

Five days before my Rizzoli screening, I visited a desk clerk friend at the Waldorf Towers, a modest hotel in New York where you can rent a suite for $2500 overnight.

George worked the midnight shift and was willing to give me twenty pieces of stationery engraved with an elegant Waldorf crest. Then I wrote a personal letter in longhand to the chief executive officer of each film company:

Mr. Joe Levine
277 Park Avenue
New York, NY 10017

Dear Joe,

Just passing through New York to London enroute from the coast. Sorry I didn't have a chance to call but I want to alert you to a marvelous new comedy feature, *Is There Sex After Death?*, that will be screened at Rizzoli's this Friday at 1:00 P.M. Don't miss it; I saw a rough cut and the picture is dynamite! Also, they need a distributor.

Give my love to the family and I'll call around Christmas.

Warm regards,
Bill

There was no last name or return address. Similar letters went out to the heads of Paramount, M-G-M, Universal, United Artists, and others.

At the appointed time, fourteen of the twenty came. Three blocks of limousines lined the curbs on Fifth Avenue.

The results were terrific. Only Joe Levine queried me about a man named Bill whom I might know. I thought about it for a moment and then decided I couldn't remember.

Theater owner Don Rugoff offered a long run at his Cinema II Theater on the East Side, where sold-out crowds brought forth a distribution agreement to book the film nationally.

How to Collect from a Deadbeat

A theater on Long Island owed film producer Robert Downey $3000 in box office proceeds for showing his successful satire *Putney Swope*.

The movie house was notorious for not paying its bills, and after months of trying to collect, the film's distributor said he could sue or save legal fees by writing off the debt as a total loss.

Downey, a man who challenges the obvious and utters the outrageous, took matters into his own hands. First, he enlisted the aid of a black actor friend who weighs 260 pounds and stands six feet, four inches. Then Raymond was fitted into a white three-piece suit and driven by chauffeured limousine to the theater.

Smoking a large cigar, he handed the shaking cashier a bill for $3000 and his business card that read:

HARLEM COLLECTION AGENCY
125th St. & Lenox Ave.
"We always collect prompt"
Open 24 hours

Raymond gruffly told her to pass along the bill to the manager and he would return the next day exactly at 5:00 P.M. for $3000 in cash. Then he gave a few mean looks to the ticket taker, blew smoke in his face, and left.

Downey heard from his distributor the next morning. The theater had sent over a certified check for $3000 by messenger, with a prior agreement that the collection agent wouldn't return.

Apparently, both the cashier and ticket taker left their jobs forever the night before.

Persistence and Proficiency Equal Prosperity

I have never understood why many great talents remain unrecognized, while far too many mediocre people often gain immediate fame and fortune.

A jazz pianist I know, who plays in the Art Tatum style, had been unable to obtain a recording contract or find a class club to showcase his exceptional talents. He spent the best years of his life giving school concerts, causing spellbound students and teachers to wonder: "If you're so great, and you are, why haven't you been discovered?"

This musical genius, Dwike Mitchell, never failed to astound audiences with his brilliant technique and incredible keyboard improvisation. Yet he remained anonymous.

When the Yale Glee Club toured Russia a few years ago, Mitchell and his bass French horn–playing partner, Willie Ruff, managed to wrangle a free trip as personnel assistants. At Moscow University, they wandered onto an empty auditorium stage one afternoon and began to play.

Within the hour every seat was filled and a rapt Russian audience heard their first live American jazz. A *New York Times* reporter who happened by filed an ecstatic story back to the States. The Mitchell-Ruff Duo became instant legendary jazz greats overseas.

Alfred Cocozza was a singer who always displayed a marvelous tenor voice, second only to Caruso, according to his parents. He endured six years of struggle moving pianos and singing from the back of his truck.

While dragging a grand piano into Philadelphia's Orchestra Hall, conductor Serge Koussevitzky heard Cocozza's marvelous voice. His encouragement, followed by an appearance in Moss Hart's Broadway show *Winged Victory,* and a name change to Mario Lanza, catapulted him to tremendous success.

My college debate teacher, Mr. Saxbe, was a graduate law student who inspired the entire class to greater heights through a process of excellence and achievement. We couldn't understand why he demonstrated his abilities in a classroom instead of the outside world.

I suspect that professor knew exactly what he was doing. William Saxbe went on to become United States attorney-general.

The Abominable "No" Men ▬▬▬

There are hundreds of thousands of junior executives and vice-presidents sitting in impressive offices. They all have something in common: the authority to say "no."

You could submit an invention worth millions or a fantastic artistic creation. The answer is always "We're not interested at this time."

The one man who can say "yes," the chairman of the board, is generally unavailable, in Europe, on his yacht, or playing golf. You are not about to bend his ears.

In just about every success story involving a television star, a winning product, or an invention, there was always a long past record of rejection.

So how does one infiltrate the closed-shop attitude? A combination of persistence, ingenuity, and performance generally pays off.

For instance, when I've been deterred by a secretary from reaching the chief executive, I call back after 5:30 P.M. when she is gone and he is more likely to answer the phone.

If the company switchboard is closed, a building guard can supply the proper nightline. And most top executives stay at their desks until seven or eight in the evening.

Once you reach him, be prepared to deliver a succinct and persuasive presentation. You might obtain an appointment, maybe even an invitation to lunch.

I tried in vain to contact Mitzi Shore, owner of "The Comedy Store" in Los Angeles, an improvisational club for comedians, to audition some new material. Her underlings informed me I didn't stand a chance. Furthermore, they were booked months ahead.

In order to penetrate their "closed door," I sent a telegram to Ms. Shore from New York:

MY DEAR MITZI,

HUMORIST ALAN ABEL WILL BE IN LOS ANGELES NEXT WEEKEND ONLY, ENROUTE TO AUSTRALIA. PLEASE ASSIGN HIM A PROMINENT POSITION ON YOUR FRIDAY NIGHT LINEUP. MANY THANKS FOR HELPING A FRIEND.

ORSON

I gambled that she would receive the wire from her "no" people and think it was either Orson Bean, the actor-comedian, or producer Orson Welles.

Arriving in Los Angeles, I called "The Comedy Store" and learned I was scheduled for the eleven o'clock prime-time evening showcase!

I was ecstatic over this coup—many deserving comedy performers can't get near the place—and my routines played well before a full house. Film producers Lane and Carol Sarasohn were in the audience and signed me to a cameo role in their next feature *Groove Tube II.*

An Antidote for Audience Apathy

Radio and television talk-show hosts often like to shake up their listeners and viewers. Increased audience ratings serve to raise advertising rates and continue a program for another season.

When people are dismayed to learn that their favorite program is being canceled, they write tons of letters. It's always too late and their gratitude should have been expressed earlier.

Radio personality Alan Douglas started in Cleveland, Ohio, and his popularity brought him to New York's WNBC. Douglas had a legion of fans for his evening talk show and he asked me to fill in one night to give his audience "a swift kick in the intellect."

My interview with recording artist and erotic actress Andrea True, allegedly in the nude, flooded the station switchboard. Angry callers demanded to know if she were really naked. The operators had no idea and I wasn't taking calls, so this heightened intrigue and established a vast tune-in audience.

Humorist Marshall Efron was also on hand, posing as a

wealthy dealer in white slavery seeking a hundred beautiful virgins.

Another time I appeared as "Omar the Beggar" on NBC–TV's "Tomorrow" with Tom Snyder. Wearing a black hood to protect my anonymity, I pretended to be the founder of a school for professional panhandlers.

Snyder attacked me on both moral and legal grounds:

"What you're teaching is immoral, Omar," he challenged angrily.

"You make personal phone calls from your office, Tom. You don't refund the money to NBC," I countered. "Do you declare taxes on your free books, booze, and other gifts? That's immoral!"

"All right," he responded, "but what you're doing is illegal. . . ."

"It's illegal to pass audible wind in a Mormon church," I interrupted. "It's illegal to make a U-turn. There are thousands of laws on the books, and if enforced we would have 200 million people in jail. I'm saving poor souls from starvation and suicide."

Our verbal battle ran for an hour on the full NBC television network and ranked as one of the top mail-pulling programs ever presented by "Tomorrow." It proved viewers get mad and want to get even.

How to Break into Television ===

During the early 1960s I wrote a fictional essay about an organization that wanted to clothe all pets for the sake of decency, namely horses, cows, dogs, cats, and any animal that stood higher than four inches or longer than six.

Known as S.I.N.A., the Society for Indecency to Naked Animals had a leader, G. Clifford Prout, who summed up his philosophy with "A nude horse is a rude horse."

A dozen magazines rejected my article and the *Saturday Evening Post* included a personal note from its senior editor: "I think this is a deplorable movement!"

That's when I decided to go directly to the public and launch a realistic clothe-the-animals crusade, using pamphlets and press releases, to dramatize my satire on the world stage.

One young actor who had the capacity to play the role of G. Clifford Prout was willing to try this tactic for a bit of notoriety. He had just returned to New York from a tour with *No Time for Sergeants* and was anxious for some television exposure.

His exceptional comedic talents were not sufficient to interest the top-rated "Tonight" Show, then hosted by Jack Paar. However, as G. Clifford Prout, a moral man with a determination to put Bermuda shorts on horses and half-slips on cows, Buck Henry was eagerly booked in rapid succession on both the "Tonight" and "Today" shows.

I pumped out realistic press releases announcing imaginary plans to picket the Washington Zoo (a public peep show) and declare the Pennsylvania Turnpike a moral disaster area (naked animals grazing nearby).

Henry was kept busy around the clock with radio, television, and newspaper interviews. S.I.N.A.'s campaign graced the front pages and became a number-one conversation piece at cocktail parties.

Eventually, *Time* and *Newsweek* reporters unmasked Buck Henry's alias and he went on to enjoy a very successful career as an actor, screenwriter, and film director.

How to Crash Hollywood ━━━━

Ted was an aspiring actor-writer-director doing rather well in New York when he decided to increase his standing by going west.

I advised him of the folly, but he persisted and spent a year in California without success, working at odd jobs to survive.

When we met in Los Angeles during one of my trips, Ted was down to $2500 in savings and a pile of scripts he couldn't give away. Agents shunned him, the studio gates were always closed, and actors were as plentiful as locusts during a plague. He was despondent and defeated.

I suggested he try one last fling before giving up and returning to New York. First, rent a Rolls-Royce, dress immaculately, and then hire an actor in a chauffeur's uniform to drive him to the major studios. His role: To negotiate renting one of their sound stages for an independent feature film based on one of his scripts.

Six weeks and $2000 into the caper, a studio head was anxious to provide his facilities and asked to read the script. Ted obliged and was offered a counter deal: he could produce and direct the film on salary, along with a share of the profits, if the studio were allowed to finance the picture rather than just rent their facilities.

Ted took the offer, the first of many more, to become an established film producer. He asked that I not use his name, but the incident is true.

The Big Payoff

Jay Clary, managing director of the Monarch Ski Lodge in Garfield, Colorado, is not a man to be trifled with. His casual manner cloaks a very shrewd business sense that has made him successful in a number of ventures. And when he has been deceived, Clary retaliates with creative clout.

One summer, a construction crew of twenty-eight men began dragging their tails finishing a swimming pool and restaurant on his property. He gave them fair warning to shape up or ship out.

The contract called for completion prior to the approaching ski season and they weren't going to make it without costly overtime.

Since the men were paid biweekly, Clary hired a Brinks truck, drove to the Denver mint, and brought back 32,000 Susan B. Anthony dollars. Each man was paid in cash.

Taking their silver loads of coins home was a minor inconvenience. The major problem came when they found that many establishments refused to accept this perfectly legal tender. That meant another burdensome bank trip for a paper-money exchange.

Clary's maneuver made news around the country and served to embarrass the local workers. It took only one more payday involving Susan B. Anthony coins before the construction work magically accelerated.

They finished on time, with a mutual understanding that final payments would be made by check.

A Belligerent Backer

During the lengthy Watergate hearings on television, my wife and I decided to speed up the laborious judicial process by creating some humorous evidence on film.

We managed to obtain video tapes of former President Nixon's speeches, and with the help of talented editor Roy Friedman, transposed the words into a rambling confession.

Mr. Nixon admitted driving the getaway car at the Watergate break-in, denied he was the father of Rosemary's baby, and urged God, the man at the top, to accept full responsibility for his sins.

Our pseudo-documentary movie, called *The Faking of the President,* was an immediate disaster at its première in Salt Lake City. The Mormon audience hooted, howled, and stormed the projection booth, forcing the theater manager to call in state troopers, after which he was chased outside and his car overturned.

The people in Utah had been violently offended at the satirical liberties taken with our ex-president's words. Subsequent bookings in colleges were a bit more successful, but theaters wouldn't touch the film because they feared similar audience outrage.

One of our backers with a $250 investment in the film hounded me for extra audits, in addition to the quarterly financial statements he received. My accountant was annoyed at having to go over the books and records every three months, meticulously explaining each expenditure.

I challenged the minority investor with a letter:

Dear Joe:

Your repeated requests for in-depth audits have been properly satisfied by my accountant and each time you expressed satisfaction.

You are entitled to this privilege in the same manner the holder of a single share of stock in any corporation can examine company records.

However, in the light of your relentless search for errors and to protect my good image for future ventures, I am now apprehensive and curious about the origin of your $250 investment.

For example, was this money earned honestly? Did any part come from questionable sources, such as gambling, unreported income, or possibly even underworld sources?

In the spirit of fair play, and with your permission, I would like to begin a trace to satisfy my curiosity. If you will kindly notify the proper bank officer at Chase Manhattan, I'll begin with him and then proceed to the bookkeeper at your office, and, finally, the Internal Revenue Service.

Additionally, I would appreciate your social security number.

Sincerely yours,
Alan Abel

Joe called me to suggest a truce. No more of his personal audits if I dropped my proposed investigation. I agreed.

Potent Postcards ▬▬▬▬▬▬▬▬

When a wealthy Chicago industrialist delayed paying a substantial debt for many months, he couldn't be reached by mail or phone. An associate covered for him by explaining, "We're experiencing a negative cash flow and you'll just have to wait or sue. We have a lawyer on retainer."

The very last comment implied that his attorney could afford to motion mine to death. I would pay endlessly for every court appearance, eventually forcing me to accept a miniscule settlement years before a trial date.

I knew the boss's home address in River Forest, Illiois, and three postcards, a week apart, began my retaliation:

Dear Charlie,

Why don't you contact me anymore? I would love to service you again but. . . .

Your everlasting friend,
Alan

Dear Charlie,

You don't return my phone calls or answer my mail. Why? Haven't I contributed *something* to your life? Please respond. I can't stand the silence much longer.

Hopefully,
Alan

Dear Charlie baby,

I'm really going out of my mind now. Don't you care about *me?* I certainly care about *you!* *Call collect,* but contact me about you know what.

> Impatiently,
> Alan

Because Charlie was quite well known, I could imagine the gossip going around the local post office.

His lawyer called and was furious over the cards. He threatened to bring them to the attention of the United States postal inspector if I didn't stop implying we were having an affair.

I explained my desire to work for Charlie again and the cards were an expression of my inner feelings, that's all. He assured me it would be a cold day in July before I ever worked for Charlie.

Finally, the outstanding debt was discussed, which he claimed to be unaware of, and I was promised an investigation.

A week later I received the full amount by certified mail.

Settle or Sue

I performed services for a major company—which shall remain anonymous to protect the guilty—and a penny-pinching new management team decided to pay only half of the balance due.

This meant not paying my bills if I accepted their deal. I called the family doctor to see if he would knock off 50%. He wouldn't. The garage mechanic, grocer, and phone company also refused.

My contract had been verbal. Contrary to what my lawyer

thinks, and people like Robert J. Ringer, I feel that a hand-shake is binding. A written contract can be breeched a hundred ways if the intent to defraud exists. I'm speaking mainly of intangible services rendered, rather than purchases, sales, or repairs.

The company offered that familiar broken-record theme: "Settle or sue."

I decided to pull the rug out from under their lofty smugness. First, I located ten products manufactured by the company and wrote the following letter to their respective advertising agencies:

Chairman
J. Walter Thompson Advertising
420 Lexington Avenue
New York, NY 10017

Dear Sir:

By way of introduction I recently performed services for the XYZ Corporation. Their new management has been unable to pay the total balance due.

In the interest of preserving their integrity and financial security, perhaps you would be willing to send a non-tax-deductible contribution to help pay off this debt. I'm sure your benevolence would be appreciated by all parties concerned.

Thanking you in advance for your generosity, I remain

Gratefully yours,
Alan Abel

I didn't have to wait long by the telephone. A company lawyer fumed and fretted at my tactic. But they paid in full promptly.

Ripped Off by an Auto Mechanic ▬▬▬▬▬

The ad said "$49.95 for a complete tune-up. Any foreign car. No kidding." I had a 1961 Mark II Jaguar that needed tuning. So I dropped it off and was told by the smiling mechanic, Norman, to give him a jingle in a week.

When I called, he was six cars behind and needed two more weeks. Also, Norman wanted to know how he should handle minor repairs. I advised that $200 was my absolute ceiling for everything, including the tune-up.

It took another three weeks before I received the joyful news: "Your baby is purring nicely and you can pick her up."

I arrived at the garage and immediately experienced a cardiac arrest when I saw the bill: $1700! Norman was unmoved as I exploded. He calmly showed me the breakdown: $49.95 for the tune-up and $1650.05 for labor and parts that included new mufflers, brakes, carburetor, fuel pump, and headlights.

He gave me two choices: a certified check for the full amount or his lawyer would procure a mechanic's lien and sell the car.

My attorney scolded me for not obtaining an agreement in writing. I explained the bold ad with its promise that disarmed my normal suspicions. Also, the small-town location in Norwalk, Connecticut, suggested a friendly trust.

His legal advice was to pay the price and take my lumps or file a suit that might require three years before trial. And I could lose.

I wasn't about to pay for unauthorized repairs and new parts. Filing a complaint with the Better Business Bureau or the district attorney was a hollow futility. The costs of a lawsuit would be expensive while my car remained stationary, requiring additional repairs from the inactivity.

My strategy was to rent a wheelchair from a hospital supply company. Then I put on an old army uniform and my wife took a Polaroid photo of me sitting in the chair looking ill and forlorn. This mood wasn't difficult to create.

The photo was reproduced on 100 circulars that read:

ARMY VETERAN VICTIMIZED!

The Classical Car Repair Shop of Norwalk, Conn., advertised a tune-up for $49.95 and I swallowed the bait. Without authorization they installed $1700 in new parts and are now holding my car for ransom. Please join the boycott against this deceptive and dishonest business.

That evening I placed circulars under the doors of every store in Norwalk, particularly gasoline stations, auto suppliers, and in bars where patrons showed a strong allegiance to a maligned army veteran.

The very next day I received an angry call from Norman's lawyer, Ray Tiernan. He warned me I faced a libel suit if I didn't stop with the circulars. I told him my defense was the truth and I'd take my chances. Furthermore, I intended to flood the state with thousands of circulars and begin picketing the garage.

My threats had a positive effect. Attorney Tiernan said he would call back within the hour. He did and we haggled over a settlement. I stood absolutely firm with $200 as the bottom line.

Four hours later the attorney advised I could pick up the car from him for $200 in cash. I requested a written guarantee that none of the parts had been tampered with or removed and he promised to supply this.

Subsequently, the garage went bankrupt when similar repair victims filed lawsuits to regain their hostage cars. And Ray Tiernan told me, a year later, that he often cited my action before his university class of law students as an example of justice without litigation.

Diplomatic Bill Collecting ▬▬

When our daughter Jennifer was two years old, I took her on a three-week lecture tour. This experience gave me the chance to feed, bathe, change diapers for, play with, and monitor a baby twenty-four hours a day, seven days a week. I learned to understand and appreciate motherhood.

There were a few embarrassing moments. I introduced her onstage at Syracuse University and Jennifer toddled out. She smiled at the applause and then made some familiar grunts while doing her duty before a hysterical audience of students and faculty members.

Aboard a plane to Atlanta, a rather large black woman sat next to us and Jennifer stared at her quizzically before announcing in a loud, high-pitched voice, "Daddy, that lady is all covered with chocolate!"

We had a tight schedule leaving Tampa, Florida, and I reached the check-in counter fifteen minutes before our evening departure to Jacksonville. The airline clerk placed our two bags on the conveyor belt and called the flight line to alert them. This was the last plane out.

With Jennifer held tightly under one arm and the other free in case we fell, I raced to the departure gate. We arrived just in time to see the attendant close the ramp and motion us back.

Furious, I demanded to know why the counter clerk's call hadn't been honored and, according to their overhead clock, the plane actually left five minutes early. Also, our bags were now airborne.

This man just gestured helplessly, gave me his business card—he was T. L. Cook, the agent in charge—and said I could come back tomorrow. He was going home.

We continued a lively shouting match and I ended with a warning that National Airlines would pay through the nose. Cook gave me a four-finger salute from the nose, much to Jennifer's delight.

Fortunately, there was a hotel in the terminal and a well-stocked drugstore. I bought all the necessary items for our overnight stay, totaling $46.70.

The following morning I paid $78.95 for the room, two meals, and long-distance calls. Then on to Jacksonville where we located our baggage and completed the rest of the tour without incident.

Was agent Cook's boss going to get an angry letter? Definitely not.

President
National Airlines
Miami International Airport
Miami, Florida

Dear Sir:

I've flown all the major airlines but National takes first prize when it comes to service. Briefly, my two-year old daughter and I missed your flight from Tampa to Jacksonville by a matter of minutes. But our bags didn't. Thanks to the humane efforts of your Tampa agent, T. L. Cook, we were graciously ushered to the nearby drugstore for required supplies and promptly checked into the airport hotel.

I am enclosing a copy of those expenditures.

Gratefully yours,
Alan Abel

The check for $125.65 arrived two weeks later with an apology for our inconvenience.

If I had vented my spleen, the company would have protected Cook by refusing to pay or, at best, offered a compromise settlement.

How to Fix a Fender-Bender ▬

While out shopping, my wife bumped a car from behind. Both vehicles were entering a ramp leading to the parkway at five miles per hour when the car ahead stopped unexpectedly.

Neither car was damaged but the other driver requested Jeanne's identification and insurance data "for the record." She suggested calling the police for an official report. He declined, saying it wasn't necessary.

Several months later his insurance company sent us a claim for $487 in repairs to be paid by our insurer. I sensed we were being set up by a "professional fender-bender." And his mechanic might even be part of such a scam.

My wife insisted there was nothing wrong with the rear of his car, nary a scratch. I believed her. So I rejected the claim on the grounds it was false, although we had no proof, such as photos or a police report. It was his word against hers and she did bump him.

I could have let our insurance company handle it, and an

exploratory call revealed that they routinely settled without an investigation. However, my wife's record would be blemished and our rates increased. This is exactly the kind of ploy that causes premiums to skyrocket.

Therefore, I suggested both parties take lie detector tests with the loser paying the cost. He wouldn't agree to this, we refused to honor the claim, and *his* insurance company finally settled for a lesser amount.

How to Punish an Insurance Company

The drunken driver failed to negotiate a curve traveling at high speed, crashed through our freshly painted red fence, knocked over four twenty-foot willow trees, tore up shrubs and fifty feet of lawn, and badly bruised three front steps.

He was unhurt and in a smiling stupor when the police arrived to issue him a citation for driving off the road, a $15 fine as opposed to more serious charges of being intoxicated.

The tipsy driver was grateful for the lesser crime and a free ride home in the wrecker that retrieved his mangled car, leaving four more deeply gouged ruts in the already-damaged lawn.

I took appropriate photos of the scene and cleaned up the debris. Four local landscapers submitted bids for complete restoration of the premises that ranged from $3500 to $4500.

When a claims agent from Fireman's Fund Insurance showed up a week later with his own appraiser, their settlement offer was $2000. I scouted other landscapers and none could see any possibility of doing the job for less than the low bid of $3500.

Two months went by as Fireman's Fund ignored my calls and letters to settle fairly. They remained firm: take the $2000 or sue.

Down from the attic came poster board, Magic Markers, and broom handles. Two signs hand-printed in bold lettering read:

WHY IS FIREMEN'S FUND INSURANCE CO. FAILING?

Then, in tiny twelve-point letters underneath: "Failing in their moral obligation to settle claims fairly and promptly."

I printed up several thousand circulars describing the accident and included a satirical essay on the folly of mating a car with a house for vicarious sexual experiences. The allegory ended with a suggestion that anyone masochistic enough to want a similar tryst should write to Fireman's Fund and arrange for an accident.

Four friends who enjoy picketing joined me on their lunch hour in front of the company headquarters in New York City. We passed out flyers as traffic slowed to a crawl while motorists blinked at the possibility a major insurance company was going under.

The picketing continued sporadically over a period of two weeks, along with anonymous calls to Fireman's Fund asking if they were really headed for bankruptcy.

On the following Monday I received a check for $3500.

Crossing Streets Safely ▬▬▬

The driver of an automobile has supreme power behind the wheel. That same person as a pedestrian often fails to appreciate the intimidation of any vehicle at a street crossing.

How many times have you stood waiting for the light to change and were then unable to cross as streams of turning cars blocked a safe passage? Then the light returned to green and you endured another long wait for the very same frustration again!

Strictly enforced California laws require motorists to yield for pedestrians at crosswalks. Other states have similar laws, but they aren't respected by drivers or upheld by the police.

Crossing a street with the light in your favor is no guarantee you'll make it because the cars turning are a real threat. It's flesh and bones against steel and plastic. There's no contest.

My solution is to carry a homemade rectangular PEDESTRIAN CROSSING sign, with black printing on yellow cardboard, mounted on a paint paddle.

Holding this sign aloft stops all traffic. It looks very official and the effect will part the waves of cars, taxis, and trucks. Even motorcycles and bicycles respect such a sign.

Should a vehicle be tempted to nudge you faster or blow its horn in protest, the reverse side of the sign is flipped to read:

UP YOURS

How to Educate a Boorish Bookkeeper

If you have an unresolved complaint with a bookkeeper over billing clarification and are unable to reach an amicable conclusion, send along this examination:

Dear Bookkeeper:

I am very concerned over your inability to understand my predicament. Therefore, would you kindly solve the following problems and return the answers to me so that I might judge your ability accordingly.

1. Mary weighs 84 pounds. The area of the soles of her feet is about 28 square inches. How many pounds does each square inch support? _____
2. Mrs. Jones had 3.2 pounds of ground beef in the freezer. She sent Bobby to the store for more. Then she had 5.9 pounds of ground beef. How much did Bobby buy? _____
3. Land covers 2/7 of the earth's surface; 1/5 of the land is in Asia. What fraction of the earth's surface is land in Asia? _____
4. George spent $2.95 for a book, $1.50 for drawing paper, and $1.25 for a pen. How much did he spend?

_____

Sincerely yours,

Contemptible Bill Collectors

The following all-purpose form letter is ideal for stalling a payment due, especially when the creditor is in hot pursuit.

Dear Sirs:

_____ Payment will be made soon.

_____ My check is about to go into the mail.

_____ My check is in the mail.

_____ I am considering bankruptcy under Chapter XI.

_____ My attorney will be in touch with you.

_____ I am presently incapacitated and will not be able to respond for at least _____ days.

_____ I have applied for a loan to pay this debt.

_____ All books and records have been stolen.

_____ Copies of your latest billing in triplicate are necessary before payment can be made.

_____ All checks must be signed by my accountant who is presently overseas.

_____ If you call once more at home, my disturbed family will require psychiatric treatment _at your expense._

_____ My associate, Bruno "The Hook" Zaparelli, will be in touch shortly to resolve this matter.

Publish or Perish

I attempted to sell a humor column to newspaper syndicates entitled "The Private World of Prof. Bunker C. Hill." The professor offered such solid ideas as "How to Live on $5 a Week," "Income Taxes Based Upon a Person's Weight," "How to Scratch an Itch in Public," and "Egg Blot Tests for Self-analysis," among others.

After about twenty rejections from the major distributors of feature material to newspapers, I figured they weren't interested.

Next I tried selling the column direct to newspapers by making a pitch to 100 of the largest dailies. There were about seven replies, all negative.

I suppose I should have given up at this point. But I recalled my college days when I had written a strong letter of condemnation to the publisher of *Down Beat* music magazine, complaining about his weak column features. In the return mail I received a challenge from the editor to put some words where my mouth was. So I did. And my column ran in *Down Beat* until I graduated.

If I were to get a hearing for my satirical columns from the key newspaper executives, I'd have to find an unorthodox method to attract their attention. What other way was there to get published outside of starting a newspaper myself? Or create such an illusion. That was the idea I pursued.

Although the *San Francisco Chronicle* had rejected my column, they were my secret target because their style was flamboyant, imaginative, and entertaining.

So, to set the trap, I mailed out a press release that announced a new California newspaper to be called the *San Francisco Times:*

FOR IMMEDIATE RELEASE

Announcement has been made by industrialist J. Donald Barker in New York that San Francisco will soon have another newspaper, *The San Francisco Times*. Full coverage of world, national, state, and city news is to be handled in an unusual manner that will permit the use of a "hardcover book" technique. Each issue will integrate all the news into a single episodic story.

For instance, Page One will begin: "The weather in the Bay Area was predicted to be fair with little change. In Washington the president called a cabinet meeting to discuss the latest Soviet threats to world peace; and while they were meeting, three liquor stores in San Mateo were robbed at gunpoint. Meantime, the stock market reported a normal amount of activity. . . ."

Full details on *The San Francisco Times* editorial staff will be announced shortly.

"J. Donald Barker" received a number of calls from the West Coast and I took the next plane out to meet with the press, radio, and television for interviews.

Three days of interrogation by the media in San Francisco left me exhausted, but on the fourth day I received a call I had hoped for. Scott Newhall, executive editor of the *San Francisco Chronicle,* invited me to lunch.

We met in the Clift Hotel dining room with his promotion manager, Phelps Dewey. They were both quite intrigued over waves of gossip rippling through the city about my new publication. I answered their questions vaguely until coffee was served:

"Gentlemen, I was on the phone with my accountant this morning and he informs me that I am in terrible financial shape. Unfortunately, the *San Francisco Times* is bankrupt before its first issue."

Both Newhall and Dewey choked momentarily, suppressing outbursts of laughter, and I went on:

"I trust you will retain this news in the greatest confidence. Now I have a problem you may be able to solve. In my enthusiasm to start the paper, I signed a new columnist, Prof. Bunker C. Hill, for two years. I'm stuck with his contract. Would you consider buying this column from me?"

Scott Newhall cleared his throat to gain some composure.

"I would be interested in examining the good professor's work," he said with difficulty maintaining a steady voice. "Do you have any samples of his column?"

Naturally I had a dozen columns, and turned them over. Newhall promised a decision the next afternoon if I could meet in his office. I did and signed a two-year contract to write for the *San Francisco Chronicle.*

Profitable Letter Writing ▆▆▆▆

Over the years I've received a staggering amount of mail from a variety of people asking advice, offering get-rich-quick schemes, or seeking information for a dissertation.

Those who respond positively to my form letter develop a healthy respect for the time, effort, and cost of replying personally.

Desk Drawer #3
234 Fifth Avenue
New York, NY 10001

Dear Sir_____ Madam_____ Other_____ :

I am sorry I cannot answer your letter personally due to the priority on my time and escalating costs as follows:

Procedure	*Minutes : Seconds*
Opening your letter	:05
Reading your letter	:30
Thinking about your letter	:20
Formulating a reply	1:50
Locating stationery	:10
Inserting paper and carbon into typewriter	:10
Typing a response	3:45
Folding, inserting, sealing	:20
Licking stamp to envelope	:05
Delivering letter to mailbox	10:15
Returning from mailbox	12:30

Total 30:00 Minutes

Materials	*Cost*
Letterhead	$.03
Envelope	.02
Onionskin	.02
Use of carbon paper	.01
Typewriter depreciation	.16
Stamp	.20
Electricity (lamp and typewriter)	.06

Total $.50

If you wish to receive a personal reply, please forward

a certified check in the amount of $7.50 ($7 for my time, $.50 in material costs). Do not ask for an open account unless you are rated in Dun & Bradstreet.

Sincerely,
Occupant

P.S. For witty or profound remarks, add $2.50.

"You Know"

I counted thirty "you knows" in a friend's five-minute telephone conversation and it was very annoying. That's one "you know" every ten seconds, at least twenty-five too many.

When I mentioned the habit, he expressed surprise and insisted he was unaware of being in this verbal rut.

A week later we talked again. Everytime he said "you know," I interrupted quickly with "I know." Finally, my tenth "I know" got to him. He stopped in the middle of our conversation with an acute awareness of the "you know" habit.

During our next discussion, he didn't utter a single "you know." But I said three and he caught me on each one, adding his own reprimand.

The next time you're bothered by a barrage of "you knows," try the "I know" retaliation. It should work.

Christmas in June ▆▆▆▆▆▆▆

A book publisher in Canada wanted to give away 10,000 expensive coffee table art books and obtain a substantial tax credit because they hadn't sold. However, when his employees tried to pass them out on Toronto streets, suspicious recipients refused to accept a free costly book.

It was mid-June and the publisher only had two weeks left to qualify for his tax bounty. We met and he expressed some anger at the reluctance of people to just take these expensive books home and enjoy them.

I offered to handle the problem and solved it in three days. Twenty men were dressed in Santa Claus costumes and the books gift wrapped in Christmas paper with all the trimmings.

Bags of books were then delivered to office receptionists by the Santas and their elves for distribution among company employees.

Each Santa Claus explained he was returning in June due to his overwhelming success the past December. Nobody refused the gifts under those circumstances!

Therapeutic Telephone Tactics ▆▆▆▆▆▆▆

A day doesn't go by that some inconsiderate secretary abruptly puts me on telephone hold for an eternity. Then I hear a click and her voice: "He's still on the other line." Click.

Now, to ease the pain, sleepy music is piped into my ear.

Nobody has asked my name or the purpose of my call. I could be the president of the United States or a friendly stranger anxious to report a fire on their floor. They couldn't care less.

Ten minutes go by, precious time wasted—and when you're over forty you really think about such matters. Another click. "He'll be right with you." Click. More music. Now a dial tone. I was cut off!

I dial once again. The line is busy. Eight tries later I finally get through to the same secretary: "Please hold." Click. Disco music, in case I care to dance.

This scenario is all too familiar to everybody, and I deplore the indignity of waiting in line on the phone without some courtesy from the overworked and underpaid secretaries.

When faced with such an intolerable situation, the best thing to do is counterattack. One way is to pretend to have a bad case of stuttering. Spend a lot of the secretary's time by slurring each syllable and consonant. She'll never be rude, put you on hold, or disconnect the line. And your call will be accurately and warmly handled.

This technique works particularly well with impatient long-distance telephone operators who want to abandon your call after six rings. Should an operator treat you rudely and you're not up to stuttering, try twisting the telephone dial for half a second on key words. This will interrupt your conversation but not disconnect the line. The effect will drive her bananas trying to figure out what's happening:

"But operator, I realize company rules don't allow you to keep ringing; however, I know they're out in the pool drowning [*twist dial for half a second*] . . . so you see how important [twist dial again]. . . . Now you must have a mother and father. . . ."

All the while you're talking non sequiturs, the phone continues ringing, the operator will stay on the line, and you've had your way, not theirs.

This latter method won't work with pushbutton telephones; so you'll have to stutter for the extra rings.

Sorry, Wrong Number

Mickey Herbst operates a busy printing firm with a telephone number one digit away from a flourishing computer sales company. On an average of twenty times a day, his phone rang with requests for computer information.

Herbst and eight employees supplied the correct number as the calls escalated and continually tied up their telephone lines. When his patience ran out, he called the computer company president, who was sympathetic but unwilling to change numbers. That is, until the erroneous calls for computers were given a rival company's phone. Then the president obtained a new listing.

I had a similar experience with customers of a fireplace shop who mistakenly dialed our home. The owner was unmoved by my complaint and advised me to endure the problem for another six months, until he could install a different telephone system.

I figured my referral number time at fifteen minutes a week for the three to five daily calls, or an hour a month. Off went a bill for $60 to cover the pending six-month period involving services rendered.

He refused to pay. I began advising callers to hurry over

to the fireplace shop for the one-day, half-price sale on everything.

Two days later we settled my account for dinner at New York's expensive "21" Restaurant.

Learning to Say "No" ══════

Magazine subscriptions by phone are everybody's pet peeve. I can advise you not to fight the pitch. Don't even wait until the plea has ended. Just say, "Yes, I'll subscribe." Then give your name, credit card number, and present bank balance as requested. Also add:

"I'm a traveling salesman, so please send the first issue to me in care of the Milford Plaza Hotel in New York; the second week I'll be staying at the Hilton in Dallas; then two weeks at the Fairmont in San Francisco; hold back the next three issues until I return from Europe. . . ."

I guarantee the sales person will hang up on you!

Telephone selling in the 1980s is to utilize computerized robots that call selected middle- and higher-income homes. Even unlisted numbers will be tapped. And you can bet, like their human counterparts, persuasive pitches will interrupt at the very moment you are eating, heading for the bathroom, or running out the door.

If you refuse to buy, you're still fair game for unwanted calls pitching products from poodle clippers to meat by mail. The subliminal selling messages are designed to wear you down, just as the third degree forces a confession from an innocent prisoner.

To eliminate these telephone nuisances for items and services you don't need or care about, try the following excuses:

1. I'm planning bankruptcy under Chapter XI.
2. The owners are away for two years and I'm house sitting.
3. I just got released from prison after serving ten years for armed robbery and dangerous assault.

For fly-by-night charity organizations and questionable religious groups seeking alms over the phone, avoid the embarrassment of refusing by offering this dialogue:

"I would like to make a substantial contribution to your cause. But first I insist that my accountant examine your books and records. Then I will write out a check as well as pay all costs for the audit."

In over twenty years and perhaps several hundred requests for funds, not a single charity or religious order has ever been willing to accept these terms!

If one of the groups had offered to open their books, I really wouldn't look. But the reluctance to "show and tell" leaves much in doubt. So I donate, instead, to the charities of my choice.

Unauthorized Long-Distance Calls

Jerry called his girl Nancy in Los Angeles from a New York pay phone and billed the charges to my number. These unauthorized bills showed up on my monthly statements in amounts ranging from $25 to $40 regularly over a six-month period.

Sorting out the illegitimate calls and documenting them became a real pain in the neck. The telephone company investigated, then said I didn't have to pay but they couldn't stop the practice . . . being too busy with more serious matters such as illegal "blue boxes."

Nancy had refused to make restitution because she didn't make the calls. Occasionally the operator would reach me to verify Jerry's charges and naturally I refused.

Once I was able to speak to him through the operator and he blatantly admitted his practice, adding: "If you're home to block my call, I'll get another operator and a different billing number."

He seemed to prefer my telephone. I knew Nancy's number and spoke with her to solve the problem. She was slippery enough to pretend innocence and would not cooperate. I was called a few unflattering names and she hung up.

Therefore, I made a few long-distance calls from a pay station to London, Paris, and Munich, billing the charges to Nancy's phone while she was at work.

It didn't take her long to pinpoint the phantom culprit, and in exactly one month Jerry stopped charging any further calls to my phone.

Obscene Telephone Calls

Obscene phone calls are more of a nuisance than a threat to one's safety. The caller requires anonymity and the telephone is his phallic symbol. Unmasked, he is undoubtedly a timid, troubled soul who needs attention and help.

Repeated and vicious calls are best referred to the telephone company so they can trace and nab the offender. If he resorts to pay stations and continues calling, I would recommend talking in a deep voice, sprinkled with loud belches. Explain with halting speech that your larynx has just

OKAY LADY YOU CALL THIS NUMBER ONE MORE TIME AND SO HELP ME I'LL BLAST YOUR PEARLS TO KINGDOM COME . . . GOT IT !
AND THIS AIN'T NO BLUFF . . . JUST YOU TRY!

been removed. This imagery should take you off the list.

If another call arrives and you answer in your natural voice, pretend you are visiting Mary who had the throat operation; then call her to the phone.

Blowing a loud whistle or even hanging up will establish your fear. Pleading or threatening to call the police suggests vulnerability and encourages the caller to try again.

Recently I was receiving a series of obscenities on my answering machine. Then I taped this reply:

"Thank you for calling. Nobody is in but you may leave a message at the sound of the beep."

After twenty seconds of recording time I concluded with: "For the particular caller who has been anonymous, a voice print is being matched with other tapes available for identification. See you in court."

My strange caller left one final message and I never heard from him again.

Telephone Answering Machines

Nothing is more exasperating than calling a friend or business and encountering the mechanical monster. Suddenly, you're "on the air" and must perform. The thirty-second tape seems like an eternity.

You are also on the hook to supply a time when you can be reached, sometimes putting a damper on taking a nap, tying up your line or going out for an errand.

Try leaving this message:

"Sorry you're not in to take my call; nor will I be available when you return. It's now 2:34 P.M., the temperature is fifty-four degrees Fahrenheit, with a north by west wind blowing east. Tomorrow should be fair. I'll call back sometime, maybe."

Naturally, don't leave your name.

For my own tape machine I have the sounds of a large dog barking and random rifle shots. Then I add:

"Nobody is here except Beowulf the guard dog and Sing Lo, my houseboy, doing some target practice before giving his class in Kung Fu. If you care to leave a message, fine. Otherwise, the same to you."

This recording has deterred random callers seeking vacant homes and apartments to vandalize. The sound effects are quite believable.

A not-so-favorite aunt never visits because she is certain we own a dangerous dog and maintain an armed guard. Salesmen, too, are reluctant to make house calls.

V.I.P. Penetration

Another telephone frustration is an inability to get through to a V.I.P. You want the boss, not his nephew, an assistant, or some other lower-level flunky. Accordingly, I recommend a pattern of dialogue as follows:

"Who is calling?"

"Dr. Abel. I would like to have a minute with Mr. Watson. . . ."

"I'm sorry, he's in conference. Let me connect you with his associate. . . ."

"But I have his x-rays."

"I'll put you right through."

"Watson here. Dr. Abel? My x-rays?"

"Not really, sir. I just wanted a minute with the top man to complain about a deterioration of your typewriter ribbons from six months' durability to about three."

Tom Watson, former chairman of the board of IBM, heard me out and promised to investigate. I was satisfied because I spoke to the boss and even received sample ribbons that did last longer.

Some executives communicate entirely by telephone. They never write letters, send telegrams, or appear in person. The telephone is their umbilical cord to the outside world. After weeks of long-distance negotiations with a Hollywood film producer who loved my screenplay, you can imagine my chagrin when he suddenly disappeared. He was never in, always out of the office, or the city, and even the country.

Finally, desperate for a resolution to his enthusiastic interest in my film story, I reported him missing to the Los Angeles Police Department. They found him that day and he liked the ploy well enough to resume negotiations.

The Talkative Telephone Nuisance

Perhaps the most annoying telephone caller is the unwelcome acquaintance who is totally insensitive to your frenzied voice.

You are in the middle of exercising, cooking, composing, writing, painting, or just meditating. But this nuisance drones on with boring trivia, never pausing to breathe, refusing you the opportunity to hang up.

Any explanation about your activity interrupted only turns on the caller, rather than suggest he or she buzz off. It's twenty minutes of frustration.

The best offensive defense is to introduce a conversation with an imaginary person in the same room:

"Listen, Tom, I really must go now and finish my symphony score for the concert tonight. . . . Oh, you played 'Chop Sticks' once in the first grade and 'London Bridge' in the third. . . . Put that chair over there, Henry. . . . Yes, Tom, I'm listening. . . . Not there, Henry, over here. That's right, now move the table; don't break the lamp. . . . What's that, Tom? Oh, Henry is my handyman. Yes, do call again when I'm not busy."

Belligerent Banks ━━━━━━━

One of the nation's largest banking systems in New York City showed no respect for its depositors. Lines extended in a maze between roped-off barriers and people on their lunch hour waited in vain. If they were lucky to make it to a window, there was no time left for eating.

While stuck in one of these abominable stalls, I was unlucky enough to reach a teller when it was time for her to shut down. She pointed me to another window where there wasn't a teller in sight. Meantime, sixteen disinterested employees wandered around.

Prepared for this occasion, I opened my briefcase and took out a sandwich and a can of soda. With a napkin carefully spread on the cage shelf, I munched away on lunch and read a copy of the *Wall Street Journal*.

Very soon, annoyed shouts from other customers brought

a teller on the run. He was ready for immediate business and loudly demanded that I accommodate him. I took my time handing over the deposit slip and checks. He then scrutinized each item and insisted I endorse the checks again in his presence, after which my signature was carefully matched with one on file.

A check to be cashed was for $86.75. When he belligerently turned over four twenties, a five, a single, and three quarters, I examined each bill meticulously, rubbed the texture to determine authenticity, bit the coins, and bounced them against the marble shelf.

As I went through this money test, the teller made a few derogatory remarks and suggested I take my account elsewhere. I decided to delay a decision until I could retaliate.

The next day my picketing comrades assembled with me in front of the bank armed with circulars and several signs reading in bold letters:

WHY IS THIS BANK SUBSERVIENT?

Pedestrians were startled at the possibility of a major bank's being subversive; that was their interpretation.

The flyers read as follows:

JOIN OUR BOYCOTT

This bank treats its customers as numbers rather than human beings. Don't just be a bystander to life, participate! Otherwise we will all spend the best years of our lives standing in line waiting for a subservient teller. Remember, it's your money, not theirs! Take this test and prove our point.

1. Have you ever been thanked for making a deposit? _____ If so, can you remember the year?_____

2. Have you ever been threatened for making a withdrawal? _____

3. Banks are in business for: _____Profit _____Hoarding _____Both

4. Would you want a member of your family to marry a banker?_____ Why not?_____

5. What is the greatest amount of time you have spent in line at this bank?_____ Hours _____Days _____Weeks

6. Banks offer free household gifts because:
   _____You need the appliances. _____They want to give you the business. _____It keeps employees occupied. _____It prevents manufacturers from going bankrupt.

7. What do banks, funeral homes, and insurance companies all have in common? _____

8. Banks refuse to open more windows during peak hours because:
   _____A long line of people makes them seem more successful.
   _____Perspiring bodies provide interior warmth and reduce fuel costs.
   _____Angry customers tend to feel insecure and deposit more.
   _____Hiring extra tellers would reduce unemployment and lower interest rates on loans.

Within ten minutes the bank manager cornered me. I forced him to walk the picket line if he wished to talk. (One of the police rules for peaceful picketing is to keep moving; otherwise they can issue a summons for blocking the sidewalk.)

He was infuriated over the signs and said our campaign was facing criminal libel. I calmly explained my beef and advised him to open more windows, teach tellers manners, or close down his operation.

At that moment a television camera crew appeared, undoubtedly alerted by a sympathetic depositor. The manager quickly shielded his face and dashed back into the safety of the bank.

We continued this charade for an hour and ran out of circulars. The manager came back when the TV crew left and promised to improve his service if we quit. We did and he kept his part of the bargain.

Snaring a Subway Thief ══════

Traveling by subway to a Forest Hills tennis game one summer afternoon, I was astounded to observe a lone youth quietly walking through the car, stripping passengers of their watches and wallets.

His switchblade was visible and nobody resisted. There were several dozen able-bodied men sitting immobilized by this punk who couldn't have been more than seventeen.

I wondered how many of these victims were possibly war veterans who had faced all kinds of danger to defend freedom. And now, in the face of a lone terrorist, they were surrendering. It was infuriating.

Casually, I wandered into the next car as the robber searched a woman's pocketbook and failed to notice my exit. Two young couples were standing by the door, oblivious of what was going on in the other car.

Both fellows were beefy and wore football-numbered T-shirts. They laughed and teased one another as I put a finger to my lips and pointed to the action in the next car. All four registered shock and just stared as I said softly:

"That guy is ripping off the passengers. And when he finishes, he said he's going to rape your lady friends."

Those two chaps bolted into the car, took flying leaps at the thug, and pounded him to the floor. Only then did other passengers join in the melee.

While frenzied scuffling and shouting continued, the train pulled into my station. I got off and went on to enjoy some tennis.

Good Highway Samaritans

One hundred fifty years ago it was easy to tell friend from foe. The enemy shot arrows, brandished a tomahawk, or fired a six-shooter your way.

Nowadays you can't be certain who is out to get you. Your disabled car might well attract a seeming Good Samaritan who ends up pulling out a gun and holding you up.

Another popular highway robbery technique is for the perpetrators to signal you off the road, pretending your left front tire is about to explode. You heed their friendly command and end up stripped of your valuables.

The more blatant road robbers will bump your car to create a minor accident, forcing you to stop and surrender your wallet.

For a lone woman driver, there is the further danger of being kidnapped and raped, perhaps even murdered.

The best deterrent against these preying monsters is a CB radio. If you can't afford that, or don't wish to risk having it stolen, install an ordinary telephone receiver with a cord that disappears under the dashboard and doesn't hook up to anything.

At the first hint of being approached by strangers while disabled on the side of the road, "telephone" the state highway patrol with an animated description of your rescuers and their car's license number.

The would-be attackers will have second thoughts about harming or ripping you off. They might even change your flat tire or repair the motor before selecting another victim.

Operation Safe Streets ━━━━━

There are over two million unregistered handguns in New York City and your chances of being attacked or robbed are probably one in four. Allowing for another two million switchblade knives, the odds are lower.

As my contribution to the "I Love New York" campaign, I recommend the following precautions:

1. Smile at the mugger and try not to make any ethnic slurs that might upset him. Soft whistling or humming is okay while you're being stripped of your valuables.
2. Always carry three or four extra cheap wristwatches and lots of one-dollar bills in a wad to make it seem like you're loaded.
3. Keep your eyes closed during the holdup so you can't identify the perpetrator. (This act will save your life, as 87% of all criminals plan to execute witnesses.)
4. When the attacker finishes with you, pretend to faint for ten minutes. Then go to the nearest church or synagogue

and give thanks for your survival. (If the house of worship is locked for protection against thieves, call Dial-a-Prayer.)

5. Don't ever enter an elevator with a stranger. Nor should you be fooled by midget crooks who look like children. If a criminal grabs you, bark like a dog and talk to yourself incoherently. Muggers are afraid of dogs and crazies.

6. If a pervert exposes himself/herself at you, laugh loudly and point a shameful finger. Flashers can't stand to be humiliated in public.

7. Don't ever *walk* to and from your hotel or apartment. Always run zigzag. It's very difficult for a sniper to hit a moving target.

8. Don't be alarmed by the extraordinary number of seedy-looking characters leering at you around Times Square. Many are actually decoy policemen just doing their duty.

How to Avoid Meat by Mail ▬▬

I couldn't get off the mailing list of a Chicago company selling meat by mail. My address plate must have stuck because I was receiving as many as a dozen of their brochures simultaneously. I wrote back several times and called once to remove my name but it didn't work.

Then they received my mailing piece:

CHEAP MEAT BY MAIL!

Constipated? There's good news for you! Now at last, the finest tidbits, leftovers from America's three- and four-star restaurants, perfectly processed

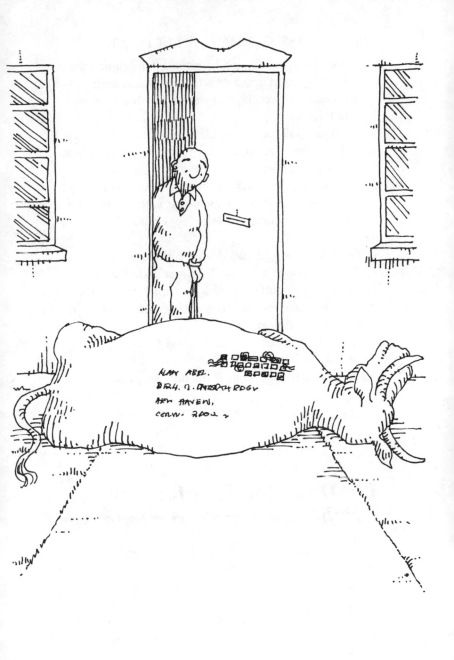

and packaged. Only $2 a pound (ten-pound mini-
mum) ground into a delectable boneless hash with
an exotic seasoning that will salivate the most bar-
ren glands.

Don't fall for fancy stuff at high prices from any
fly-by-night Chicago firm when you can dine like
royalty on *Heavenly Hash!*

Our grinders and mashers are working twenty-
four hours a day to supply you with the best for
less. Send your order in today without delay!

The sales manager called me from Chicago.

"Is this garbage or a gag?" he demanded angrily.

I soothed his ruffled nerves by explaining it was a trial
balloon, that we intended to go public, and I offered to buy
a list of his customers.

He refused, naturally, and insisted I remove their name
from our mailings. I requested the same courtesy and he
agreed to personally destroy my address plate.

Lie Detector Test for Politicians

Political mailings can become a real nuisance. After piling
up a box of several hundred pieces, I realized many of the
postage-paid return envelopes could be put to good use;
namely, sending back the following *Lie Detector Test.*

Only a few brave souls in Congress have had the gumption
to reply . . . some with humor and a further plea for my vote
or donation.

LIE DETECTOR TEST

Important! This is an acid test and must be taken quickly. Place a piece of blue litmus paper under your tongue, close your eyes, and answer all questions honestly, preferably out of both sides of your mouth. Go!

1. Do you swear to tell the whole truth and nothing but the truth? _____

2. Would you care to reconsider your answer to the last question? _____

3. Do you have any relatives presently serving on your payroll? _____

4. Define nepotism: _____

5. So far how do you like the test? _____

6. Is your laundry done in Washington?_____ The Bahamas?_____ Switzerland?_____

7. What brand of gasoline do you buy?_____ Exxon? _____Gulf? _____Texaco? _____Mobil?

8. If you were to receive a corporate campaign donation, would you prefer that it come from: _____Exxon? _____Gulf? _____Texaco? _____Mobil?

9. Have you ever been photographed kissing a potential voter?_____ Did you enjoy the experience?_____ Explain: _____

10. If you were involved in an ABSCAM-type scandal, would you rather be exposed by: _____The FBI _____Jack Anderson _____Rona Barrett

11. *Problem:* A police escort is waiting to rush you from your office to one of the following locations. Which *one* would you choose?

    _____Your wife's unexpected arrival at the airport after spending six months in an Iranian prison.

    _____Your aged mother found sitting in the local

bus station suffering from amnesia.

———— A $1000-a-plate fundraising dinner in your honor, attended by 400 wealthy businessmen, and you are already an hour late.

12. What question would you like to see added to this test? ————————————

The Dumb Dumb Letter

You correspond with a firm and receive replies that consistently evade the issue presented. They ignore your pleas and threats for an intelligent response.

It is time to send a "Dumb Dumb Letter," handwritten with a liberal sprinkling of mistakes and errors. I guarantee you will be promptly pacified.

Dear Sirs:

As you now I have been tempting to solve our problim over the weeks and months with know sucess. You seem too fail too gasp my point.

I would like to see this mater now termate so I dont write you continously at expence on my party. I already got $17 in stamps and calls and I still feel lousy.

I woud like to spend a few hours with you and key execs to help shutup my problem.

However, I must recieve wage for time and energy, not more than $200 wich will include grub and travel gas.

I have mobil home for sleep and can park overnites in your lot.

Let me look forwrd to any reply or my arrival on Monday, whichever comes sooner.

Your sincere customer,

Provoking a Priggish Person ▬

You've written a company for precise information, enclosed a self-addressed envelope, and all you get back is a form letter that checks off some lame reply.

A follow-up letter brings another computerized excuse. You call for clarification and are shuttled from office to office, cut off a few times, and then told to write again.

When you finally insist on speaking with a responsible person, he or she asks for more details. You supply them. Three weeks later another form letter arrives and you are ready to commit homicide.

Instead, provoke the general manager with *your* form letter:

RETURN THIS FORM WITHIN 48 HOURS
(All questions must be answered)

1. In 25 words or less, describe your early toilet training:
2. Do you practice oral gratifications such as:
   _____Smoking? _____Fingernail biting?
   _____Tooth picking?
3. Have you ever been accused of child abuse?_____
   Wife beating?_____ Indicted?_____
   Convicted?_____ Exonerated?_____
4. Do you fear experiencing mental pause during your life?
   _____
5. Every company has its internal pecking order. Do you consider yourself: _____A big pecker? _____A medium-sized pecker? _____A small pecker?
6. What is your I.Q.? _____50 _____75 _____100
7. Estimate your secretary's I.Q.: _____75 _____100
   _____125

8. If the big boss called you an S.O.B., would you hit him? _____ Where? _____

9. If you are fired for incompetence, would you consider working as a: _____Messenger? _____Pants presser? _____Dish washer?

10. On your last job, were you ever caught with your hand in the till?_____ About to enter the till?_____ Having just left the till?_____

11. Have you ever checked into a hotel or motel under an assumed name?_____ Why?_____

12. What is the most valuable part of your body? _____ Is it insured?_____ How much?_____

13. Do you suffer from indecision? _____Yes _____No _____Maybe

14. *True or False:* Castration is a form of government in Cuba: _____

15. On a scale of one to ten, rate yourself in the following categories:

Category	Points
Nebbish	_____
Eunuch	_____
Paranoid	_____
Nerd	_____
Jackass	_____
Ratfink	_____
Scumbag	_____

16. Describe any history of leprosy, syphilis, idiocy, or mental illness in your family:
(Use backside if necessary.)

Solving a Crisis Simply ▬▬▬▬

After a year of negotiations with the Grand Trunk Railroad, I acquired a seventy-year-old caboose to present our four-year-old daughter, Jennifer, as a playhouse.

This unusual railroad car was delivered to a siding four miles from my home in Connecticut, and I casually approached the local Zoning Commission for a permit "to install a playhouse in our backyard that resembles a caboose."

Four eagle-eyed commissioners raised their eyebrows and further questions. The forty-ton weight, fifty-foot length, and fifteen-foot height suggested to them it was actually a caboose.

I argued vehemently over the semantics of a playhouse's definition. In spite of a petition by neighbors approving the caboose, a permit was denied because of our residential zone.

Jennifer was heartbroken but I explained we could appeal the following week before the same board.

"What are you going to do if they say no?" I asked.

"Cry," she said.

"That's it," I advised. "And don't stop until they change their minds."

I didn't have high hopes for this approach. Other residents, such as Paul Newman and Joanne Woodward, had gone to court when the appeals board denied their request for a dance studio. Litigation was out because the caboose had to be removed from its temporary siding within thirty days.

Jennifer and I entered the appeals session on a Thursday evening and waited among several dozen contractors and homeowners seeking building permits. When called, our caboose was rejected by the chief commissioner.

I gave her a knowing look and Jennifer burst into tears, sobbing openly and loudly. People in the outer room peeked through the door, hearing a child in distress.

As the wailing continued nonstop, four embarrassed men fidgeted, unprepared for this outburst.

"Jennifer," I said sternly. "That's enough. You are *not* going to have a caboose!"

I wiped her tears, the commissioners held a whispered huddle, and the leader said, "All right, Jennifer, you can have your playhouse."

She gave each man a kiss and they were all smiles.

Next step, moving the caboose. The contractor with the heavy equipment necessary estimated a cost of $2000 for two flat-bed trucks, a giant crane, and an eight-man crew.

This posed a real financial problem, so Jennifer and I visited Louie Gardella's office with her piggy bank and she handled the negotiations.

"Mr. Gardella, my daddy and I have talked. But I only have the money in my bank. If you bring my caboose home, I'll let you play in it."

"How much do you have in there?" he asked, charmed by her innocence.

While I remained stoically silent, Jennifer opened the bank and counted out $4.61 in coins. Gardella did some figuring on his calculator.

"Jennifer, if your daddy will loan you $395.39, we'll do a $400 job just for you."

Another kiss, another solution. The caboose was delivered without mishap and Gardella's crew enjoyed a party afterward as flocks of neighborhood children danced around their first old-fashioned, life-size caboose.

Obviously, a youngster can be very useful for overturning board decisions and solving a budget crisis.

ABEL & ABEL

VS

THE STATE OF CONNECTICUT

Group Traveling

Rich Szabo, a jazz trumpet player and leader of an eighteen-piece band, travels by chartered bus during concert tours and has to overcome the difficult task of feeding his hungry troupe at crowded turnpike restaurants.

His solution is to supply each musician with a black mourning armband. Then they file into the restaurant and are given prompt service.

Another hangup with traveling groups is checking into a hotel. There is often an eternal lobby wait while trainees struggle with assigning rooms to waiting businessmen. Nobody seems to care.

The resolution here, if you're not accommodated in a reasonable amount of time, is to hold a group prayer session in the center of the lobby with appropriate hymn singing.

When Betty Boop ran for president of the U.S.A. in 1980, our twenty-member entourage was told we had an hour wait before a Las Vegas hotel could handle our check-in. That is, until the strains of "Come to Jesus" echoed through the gambling tables; then three desk clerks dropped their pens and personally whisked us to our rooms.

Traveling overseas with groups can offer additional headaches because some foreigners resent the so-called affluent Americans arriving on their soil. You are forced to wait for accommodations, dining, and boarding transportation.

Former travel counselor Frank Murgalo overcame this frustration by seeking out the person in charge and explaining that his people were all former mental patients, and that they would become disturbed if forced to wait another minute.

Occasionally a tour group on an airplane will be asked to

disembark in favor of full-fare passengers. I was aboard one such flight and, as group spokesman, refused to budge. Four security guards returned to carry out a possible physical eviction. I cited various congressional amendments, the Geneva Convention, and a $50,000 skin rash from each of us. We were allowed to stay, accompanied by applause from other passengers.

Feisty Friends

Richard Berlowe owns a kitchen cabinet business in Cranford, New Jersey. An unscrupulous competitor began to imitate his newspaper display ads, call him with fake orders, and try to hire his salesmen.

Berlowe retaliated by placing a classified ad in the local papers asking for women to type at home or take telephone orders, and he listed his competitor's number. The hostilities ended quickly.

Another enterprising fellow is Paul Hiatt, an aspiring writer determined to succeed at his craft in spite of a low income and spiraling expenses. To avoid paying for an unlisted telephone number, he chose a name from a cemetery. All of his bills are paid in cash, with sacks of pennies, so he is never welcome to meet his financial obligations on time. And whenever Hiatt has been ripped off by a sleazy product, he advertises for similar victims to unite. Then they sue together in Small Claims Court.

Michael Rothschild is an Atlanta recording company executive with a sinus condition that flares at the slightest whiff of smoke or any toxic fumes. When a smoker is puffing in his direction, Rothschild will pretend to blow his nose vigorously and continuously with a single finger, while creating a loud swishing sound. If that doesn't move the smoker, he is capable of simulating a series of wet sneezes that spray saliva into the air. Smokers will risk inhaling tar but they can't take unidentified flying germs.

Simon Bond, the illustrator of this book, is offended by people who suck their teeth after dining. His retaliation is to take out a nail clipper and begin trimming a table partner's toenails.

Newt Mitzman, a New York advertising executive, always manages to subdue the violator in a no-smoking section of a restaurant or train by carrying an airline sickness bag. He approaches the smoker, bag open, with a pained expression on his face.

Sandy Robinson, a Pittsburgh industrialist, ends restaurant smoking in his vicinity by feigning a respiratory attack. Placing a wet napkin around his throat, he staggers to the smokers' table. They are always willing to cooperate by dousing their cigarettes.

A Compendium of Aggravations and Retaliations

1. *Your $25 check bounces even though you have advance checking funds available. The bank will credit you for the overdraft charges and sometimes send a form letter of apology. But the damage has been done.*

   Purchase a small gift for the annoyed payee . . . around $10 . . . and bill the bank with an explanation. They will honor the expense.

2. *A credit-card company orders you to put a check in the mail immediately or they will cancel your account within seventy-two hours. And it's a week until payday.*

Send the check without a signature. By the time it's returned and signed, you will have gained two weeks to deposit the necessary funds.

3. *You have a one-hour lunch break and the line at the bank is forty-five minutes long. It is crucial to cash a check and make a deposit. The bank officer turns a deaf ear to your plea for immediate service.*

Flash a used airline ticket before another bank officer and explain the urgency of catching your plane. He will personally run behind the cage to handle all transactions.

4. *A fair-weather friend at work always needs a "fast twenty" until payday and the loan remains unpaid for weeks. You're embarrassed to badger the piker and it's even more uncomfortable because your desks are close together.*

Keep an extra billfold with three singles and some loose change. Empty it on your desk and explain: "Here are my assets, friend; I was just about to hit you for a loan." For the next request, produce a bounced check from the same wallet to establish your insolvent position. The third time, show an empty wallet with an IOU for $50 owed to your aunt. Thereafter, you should become a poor lending risk.

5. *A company owes you a few hundred dollars and keeps promising to pay but never does. Three months have gone by and you need the money desperately.*

Locate an actress through a talent agency who can shed tears on command. She visits the company office wearing shabby clothes and hands a bill to the receptionist for the general manager. When he appears to explain that they don't do business this way, she breaks into tears and sobs: "My boss said I would be fired if I don't come back with a check." Rules will be broken to save this poor girl's job.

6. *A tightwad relative worth mountains of money dangles his carrot with constant reminders that "The will can be changed if you don't mind your Ps and Qs."*

Find a promising venture or investment and request an unsecured loan against your inheritance with the explanation: "I want to enjoy the benefits of your generosity while you are alive. After you're gone it won't have any meaning." If this showdown doesn't work, be prepared to receive a token $1 because the ASPCA is getting it all anyhow.

7. *A habitual book borrower never returns them on time, if at all.*

Paste a card in the back of the book that shows the date borrowed. Include a notice: "If unable to return within ten days, please forward the cover price of book plus tax."

8. *A nosey neighbor drops by at the wrong time for morning coffee and intends to stay for lunch too.*

Prearrange a word code signal with a friend and call him or her when your patience has been tried. They will call you back in ten minutes posing as "your lawyer who is on his way over to discuss a legal matter."

9. *Door-to-door salesmen who require only five minutes of your time.*

Keep a "Tag Sale" sign in the vestibule closet. Bring it out and explain you are selling everything for a move to Australia.

10. *An obnoxious telephone call from a creditor, relative, or other parasite.*

Smell something burning and take your time fixing it. Or announce a delivery at the front door. (Rig a switch near the phone so you can ring your own doorbell.)

11. *You've taken a number to be waited on in the market and missed your call. The clerk shrugs helplessly and ten people behind you will be served first.*

Develop a slight fainting spell and request immediate service. (Next time, take two numbers for insurance.)

12. *You have a confirmed seat on an airline and they won't let you aboard because the flight has been overbooked and filled to capacity.*

There are laws that force the airline to place you on another flight within several hours and/or pay a bonus for your plight as well as a free flight. However, if you must be on that particular departure and nobody will give up a seat, you can demand, and often receive, a private plane for the trip.

13. *You are terribly allergic to smoking inside your house. In spite of this knowledge and a lack of ashtrays, some people won't respect your condition.*

Place several extra smoke alarms around that are easily activated at the first whiff of smoke. For added dramatic effect, install a fire bell and start the clanging when necessary.

14. *Your complaining letter to a company concerning a defective product or shoddy services receives only a semipolite response and no promise for making good.*

Write a stronger letter with your plan to contact all friends and business acquaintances not to patronize them if they don't make proper restitution within forty-eight hours. At the bottom of your letter, add "cc" (carbon copy) to a variety of news sources such as Associated Press, United Press International, and local newspapers, radio, and television news departments. Also, the Better Business Bureau, Chamber of Commerce, and Department of Consumer Frauds. Somebody will begin cracking a whip in your favor.

15. *An inconsiderate person plops down on the beach and loudly plays a radio that blasts a few dozen peaceful sunbathers.*

Quietly move among the people being disturbed and

form a posse of eight. Then surround the unpleasant one and offer two choices: turn the radio off or it will be taken out to sea and drowned.

16. *Every theater audience contains a few clods who talk and ruin the film dialogue as though they were at home watching television.*

    If you are with a group, at the count of three, everybody shout "Shhhhhhhh!" If that doesn't work, during a lull in the movie, utter one loud blood-curdling shriek. The usher will come running and hang around to discourage further disruptions. Should the ill-mannered patrons be near you and refuse to shut up, begin talking loudly to your partner when they talk; stop only when they do and continue accordingly. This interference will disturb them and everyone else in the theater, leading to a general uprising and a total truce.

17. *You've paid a bill in cash, can't find the receipt, and are being badgered for payment. Furthermore, nobody in accounts receivable is willing to solve the problem.*

    Document the time, date, and place the money was paid. Then send your own bill for the *loan* of this money plus interest at the prevailing rate.

18. *Someone has maliciously entered your name for a magazine subscription and the circulation department isn't honoring your repeated requests to stop sending more issues and bills.*

    Send your final complaint in a special-delivery letter bearing only a one-cent stamp with no return address. The circulation department will have to pay $2.29 postage due. Repeat this process until the problem is solved.

19. *An employee has verbally abused you without justification, perhaps even used some physical force but not enough to cause bodily harm, only mental anguish.*

    Write a detailed letter to the attorney-general's office in Washington asking for an investigation to determine

if your civil rights have been violated, subjecting the offender, upon conviction, to a ten-year jail sentence, a $10,000 fine, or both. Send a carbon copy to the employee's boss.

20. *Some obnoxious person you hear from every three years has written to see if you're still alive and announces you'll be visited shortly.*

Reseal the letter, mark "moved" on the envelope, and forward to any address in another city. It will be returned to the sender stamped "addressee unknown."

21. *You are generally ignored at social gatherings. If there was only some way you could be the center of attention just once. . . .*

At the next cocktail party, take along twelve hard-boiled eggs. Then, while mixing and making small talk, surreptitiously drop an egg into a person's purse or pocket. Eventually, as the eggs are discovered, hilarity will prevail and the culprit honored with unprecedented attention.

22. *A friend or relative you could live without sends a rotten gift at Christmas or on your birthday.*

a. Gift wrap one glove and send it.

b. Mail a gift certificate from a store that has gone out of business.

c. Send one ticket to a Broadway show that closed opening night.

d. Rewrap the gift received and send it to the donor as yours.

23. *Your dinner party ended four hours ago but the guests still haven't taken strong hints to leave.*

a. Start a prearranged argument with a member of your family; shout, scream, and throw a few cheap dishes into the fireplace. Continue the fight in another room.

b. Announce there will be group sex, seize your partner, and begin some torrid preliminary foreplay.

24. *Neighbors in the apartment next door play loud rock music early in the morning or late at night, refusing to tone down the volume.*

  a. Obtain a sound-effects recording of a dentist's drill and play it loudly against the wall until you win a truce.

  b. Buy a Morse Code key, amplify the sound ten times over a public address system, and practice your S.O.S. late at night.

  c. Invite friends over for group chants and primal screaming. Record the session and play it back as necessary.

  d. Rent a twenty-eight-inch bass drum and practice marching band tempos with a wooden beater at odd hours.

25. *A stranger sitting next to you on a bus, train, or plane reads your newspaper over your shoulder.*

As you finish each page, tear it off and hand it to him. If he refuses to accept it, tear the page into small pieces and store them under your armpit. The stranger will stop reading and change seats.

26. *A rude waiter is busy socializing with other employees and ignores your pleas for service.*

Print "SERVICE PLEASE!" on a napkin and hold it high above your head to attract his attention. If the waiter expresses annoyance at being summoned, for good measure leave lipstick smears on napkins and glasses at a nearby table. New customers will scream bloody murder at the waiter.

27. *Ill-mannered kids playing in your house or apartment have broken items that will have to be repaired and paid for.*

Surround the kids with tools and the damage; take a Polaroid picture of the mess and send it home with them and a note: "We tried to fix things but didn't have much success." You'll receive an offer to pay for the repairs and retain their parents' friendship as well.

28. *The airline has lost your baggage and you've arrived at the hotel without a stitch of extra clothes or a toothbrush. It may be hours or days before the bags are discovered.*

     Make a list of every single item and estimate the costs, totaling at least $2500. Call the airline general manager and inform him you intend to purchase *everything* on the list at their expense in two hours. Your bags will be discovered miraculously and delivered promptly.

29. *Your roof leaks after an expensive repair job and the contractor doesn't want to make good.*

     Post a visible sign on the roof as follows:

THIS ROOF HAPHAZARDLY REPAIRED BY
(name of contractor)
AND IT STILL LEAKS!

30. *You would like to spend a nice quiet day at home but the doorbell keeps ringing.*

     Quickly put on your coat and answer the door; depending on who it is, you're either on your way out or have just arrived.

31. *Your grades in college aren't up to par and dad has threatened to stop sending further funds.*

     Send him a promissory note for the sum required to finish school, payable when he retires along with your eternal love and companionship.

32. *A questionable friend constantly puts you down for your lack of taste in clothes.*

     Send him or her a burlap bag as a gift on an appropriate day such as Christmas, Valentine's Day, or his/her birthday.

33. *You've returned from vacation and your place has been vandalized. You can't afford an expensive alarm system.*

     Rig a series of tiny red light beams that crisscross windows and doors in perpendicular lines. Thieves will assume you are wired for detection and won't risk breaking the contact. Also, obtain a prerecorded tape of dogs barking intermittently on a continuous loop and play this back when you're away for any period of time.

34. *Your civic leaders have been unwilling to respond to a variety of problems that affect the community and letters to them are ineffective.*

Print up a letterhead that reads: "Citizens to Remove Incompetent Politicians (C.R.I.P.)." Obtain a post office box number, appoint yourself director of C.R.I.P., and write a strong letter as representative of thousands of angry voters. Action will be forthcoming.

35. *While standing in an overcrowded bus or train, a stranger has taken a fancy to your body and is probing for pleasure.*

Rather than face the embarrassment of ordering the person to stop bothering you, shout, "A mouse, a mouse!" and jump up and down. You'll get additional leg room and the masher will be out of business. If not, keep feeling more mice.

Conclusion

Hopefully, this book will serve a useful purpose toward motivating a vast majority of people who have been repeatedly stepped on and remain apathetic.

Even if you don't declare all-out war on the intimidators, consider taking an occasional pot shot based on the successful experiences between these covers.

Forget physical violence or criminal actions; instead, only deserving revenge delivered with dedicated style and a sense of humor to defend your honor.

Start by paying a loathsome debt in pennies. Or picket the cleaners who ruined your garment. Don't hesitate to use Small Claims Court for legitimate beefs against corporations.

By law, an attorney must defend them; you are allowed to represent yourself and the judge's decision generally favors an underdog.

When American Express messed up my credit-card account, I charged them $300 for six months of correspondence and extra bookkeeping. Small Claims Court ruled in my favor.

So, *don't get mad . . . get even!* You'll sleep sounder, breathe easier, save money, and live a longer, more tranquil life.

The Author

Alan Abel is best known for his satirical spoof, S.I.N.A., the Society for Indecency to Naked Animals, a tongue-in-cheek crusade that pretended to clothe all pets for the sake of decency.

As Omar the Beggar, he captured worldwide media attention with a school for professional panhandlers that never existed, except in his mind.

He also promoted political campaigns for phantom presidential candidates Mrs. Yetta Bronstein, Sam Silverstein, and Betty Boop.

Abel has appeared on numerous national television programs and his zany escapades have been widely published.

Recently, he starred in a critically acclaimed Broadway show, *Jester at Large,* and presently teaches a comedy workshop at the New School.

Illustrator Simon Bond is the author of two bestselling books, *101 Uses for a Dead Cat* and *Unspeakable Acts.* He divides his time between London and Phoenix while writing an original motion picture comedy.